A HIKING AND CAMPING GUIDE TO THE

Flat Tops Wilderness Area

Al Marlowe

Fred Pruett Books
2928 Pearl
Boulder, CO 80301

All of the trail maps shown in this book are reproductions of sections of topo maps published by Trails Illustrated, PO Box 3610, Evergreen, CO 80439-3425. It is our recommendation that you obtain the actual maps for trail use.

WARNING: There can be risks attendant with hiking and camping at high altitude. This guide is not a substitute for the user's judgment and personal responsibility. The trail descriptions in this guide have been carefully prepared from first hand experience. Some trails are subject to change by private or government action. You alone are responsible for coming prepared with proper equipment, experience, and common sense.

To Melvin,
my Golden Retriever and constant companion
for seven of his eight years;
he enjoyed our trips to the Flat Tops.

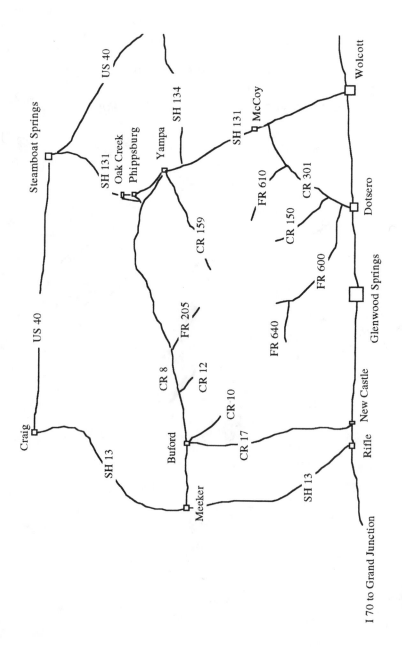

Road map to Flat Tops Area

Table of Contents

Indian Cliffs Trail
Canard Creek Trail
Bear Park Trail
East Fork Trail
Red Dirt Trail
West Sweetwater Trail
Trail 1839
Crossing Trail
Broken Rib Trail
Grizzly Creek Trail (North)
Hanging Lake Trail
Grizzly Creek Trail (South)
No Name Creek Trail

Preface

When I first visited the Flat Tops Wilderness, I had no idea the experience would eventually lead to this guide. I also had no idea of the special nature of the area. A neighbor mentioned that he and a few friends were going to fish a place called Lost Lake and that I might want to go along. A group of five people more unprepared for the wilderness would be hard to imagine.

We used an air photo for navigation since no detailed topos were then available. One of us may have had a compass but I don't recall. For our overnighter, each angler had a sleeping bag. Our packs were a hiker's nightmare, containing assorted equipment of questionable suitability. For cooking, one single-burner stove and a wood fire served to prepare, actually to burn, our meals. One camper insisted on carrying an iron skillet and 16-cup coffee pot. No one had a tent. Our shelter consisted of a plastic painter's drop cloth draped and tied over brush and poles. During the night, the painter nearly wrecked our shelter while dreaming that a bear had attacked us. The fishing wasn't that great, either. Only one fish, though it was a nice one.

That first excursion in 1969 led to other summers and additional explorations of the wilderness. Since that time, I have hiked, backpacked, ridden horses, fished, hunted, photographed, and camped in the wilderness and surrounding areas, and visited many of the lodges. Five and six trips per year have been normal. With each visit, I discover something new, something that gives me an excuse to plan another trip.

Since that summer weekend twenty five years ago, I have had the pleasure of visiting the wilderness with family and many friends. Karl, my son, and Jean, who is Mrs. Marlowe, have accompanied me on many trails. Larry Stankiewicz and his family from Littleton accompanied the Marlowe family on our first visit to Trappers Lake. Our daughter Karol was along for that trip, her only visit to the Flat Tops. Kip Wilson, another resident of the flatlands of Littleton, and Randy Smith and Ron Belak, both Evergreen anglers, shared their backpack camps with me. Ken and Carol Rupkalvis drove up from San Antonio to accompany Jean and me on our first backpack of 1993. For four days, we slogged through high water and snow to camp at Marvine Lake in mid-June. John Murphy, Bob Clark, Jay and Pierce Garton, and Bob Bockholt have all shared hunts in the Flat Tops, both successful and unsuccessful. Tom Piccirilli and Don Decicco, friends from Lakewood, shared their knowledge of the wilderness with me, pointing out areas of interest that would not have been obvious.

Three friends who tagged along on visits to the wilderness enjoyed the area even though they had little understanding of the significance of the Flat Tops. Melvin and Matilda, our Golden Retrievers walked many miles of trail and stream and helped keep Jean and me warm at night. Melvin wasn't around to accompany us in ' 93 as I had planned. Skipper, our youngest Golden, experienced his first backpack hike at just over three months of age. By summer's end, he had hiked more than 100 miles in the wilderness.

Wilderness Rangers from the Yampa District also contributed their expertise. John Anarella, Eric Petterson, and Jeff Hovermale all willingly shared stories of the Flat Tops history and offered suggestions regarding caring for and respecting the wilderness. I am also indebted to Ron Taussig from the Blanco District and Kathy Shoup from the Eagle District for reviewing and correcting the trail descriptions in their districts.

My thanks also go to several businesses that supported this work. Patrick Smith, who designs and builds those great Mountainsmith backpacks, made it possible for Jean and me to carry our gear with ease. Well, at least as easy as it's possible with forty five pounds on our backs. Mary Kay and William L. Stoehr furnished the Trails Illustrated maps for the guide. Fred Wilson of Buck Knives, Inc. supplied equipment for the 1993 season, too.

Editing is probably the most tedious and time consuming part of writing. Special thanks go to Jean, who reviewed this work several times. Donna Watson, Karen Duvall, Brendan Reidy, and Peter Graebner, friends and fellow scribes, all critiqued this work in its formative stages. Also, thanks to Dr. Paul Auerbach, of Stanford University Hospital, and Dr. Tom Morgan, and Peter Kummerfeldt for reviewing the section on altitude related illness.

The one person who's dream became the wilderness, unfortunately, we are unable to meet in person. Arthur Carhart worked for the newly formed Forest Service in the early 1900s. It was his desire to see the Trappers Lake area preserved. He lived to see his dream eventually became reality with the passage thirty years ago of the Wilderness Act. Without Carhart's foresight, Trappers Lake, and possibly the entire wilderness, would be just another development rather than the unique area it is. Without Carhart's dream, I would have nothing to say about the Flat Tops.

Chapter One

The Flat Tops Wilderness Area, located in west-central Colorado, is about 150 miles west of Denver. It is a popular destination for both residents and out of state visitors. It is bounded by Interstate 70 on the south, State Highway 13 on the west, Rio Blanco County Road 8 on the north, and State Highway 131 on the east. The Flat Tops Wilderness is the second largest in the state, covering 267 square miles spread across four counties: Eagle, Garfield, Rio Blanco, and Routt. The boundaries fall within two national forest: White River and Routt. Several hundred miles of trails provide access to the area.

This wilderness is unique. It compares with no other mountain range in the state. Only the Columbia Plateau of the Pacific Northwest is similar. There are no tall spires, and no fourteeners are found in the Flat Tops. Rather, it is a massive block of rock pushed upward and planed level, its surface punctured here and there with rare peaks rising a thousand feet above the high plateau.

The land doesn't challenge you the way other mountain ranges will. There are few steep-sided peaks. At an average elevation near eleven thousand feet, it doesn't starve you of oxygen as climbing a fourteener would. Still, this second largest wilderness in the state is not without its own special challenges. A visitor could spend an entire season in the Flat Tops and not hike every path.

From a distance, the Flat Tops Wilderness lives up to its name. Travelling along State Highway 131, between the communities of Toponos and Yampa, the plateau to the west appears to be nearly flat. Here and there, incisions were made in the massive block, formed by stresses deep within the earth during the formation of the Rocky Mountains. Rivers and creeks that drain the land enlarged and deepened the cuts.

Along the west flank of the White River Uplift, the geologic name for the Flat Tops, sedimentary rocks have been folded. Solid rock and overlying sediments deposited by ancient seas were pushed upward by forces of plate tectonics. The sediments conformed to the core rocks in the same way a bedspread drapes a bed. At the edges, the rocks were folded. At a rate imperceptible in a single lifetime, the exposed sediments eroded, then were swept away by wind and rain, leaving only remnants of folds along the west flank of the Flat Tops. You will find this uplifted, folded, and eroded structure, known as the Grand Hogback between State Highways 13 and 325 near Rifle Gap Reservoir north of Rifle. Along Interstate 70 between Glenwood Springs, and New Castle, red sediments sloping steeply to the south, give additional testimony to the forces that built the Flat Tops.

Each year, 170,000 visitors come to the wilderness and surrounding area. They come in all seasons for a variety of reasons. Some visit the many excellent wilderness-style lodges. Many come for the fishing and hunting. Backpackers and horsemen travel the trails in the backcountry. And while the number seems large, as in many places in the back country, if you get any distance from edges and trailheads, you encounter fewer people, allowing each individual or group the privacy desired.

History

The written record of the Flat Tops is sparse. Early Spanish explorers travelled the southern and western areas of the state. The Zebulon Pike and Stephen Long expeditions explored east of the Rockies. The westward migration that began following the exploration of the Louisiana Territory took several routes, all of which passed either north or south of the Flat Tops. Very little, if any record exists of early American or European explorers venturing into the area other than a few fur trappers.

It is thought by some that humans first used the area about 10,000 years ago. Ute Indians were the most recent Native Americans to inhabit the Flat Tops. For more than two centuries, they travelled and hunted from southern Wyoming as far south as Taos, New Mexico. Having acquired horses by 1740, they could easily venture into the plateau to hunt.The Forest Service has marked many trails travelled by the Utes.

The region was settled by Whites in the mid-19th century. In 1878, Nathan Meeker was appointed agent for the White River Agency, located near the town that bears his name. His ambitious but ill-advised plan to reform the Utes, changing them into farmers rather than wandering hunters, ended in disaster. Chief Douglas and 25-30 Utes set fire to the Agency on the White River on September 29, 1879, killing Meeker and ten other men. Major Thomas T. Thornburgh brought a small force of 153 soldiers from Fort Steele, Wyoming too late to protect the agency. Near Milk Creek, northeast of town, Chief Colorow and nearly 400 Utes ambushed the force, killing Thornburgh and 12 soldiers. Even though the Indians won the battle, they lost the war when the army moved them to a reservation in Utah three years later.

Geology

As a historian pores through old writings, putting together a story, the geologist studies the record of the Flat Tops in the rock. The story tells, if you listen, of the history; how this area came into existence, what makes it unique. It is a story that begins nearly three billion years ago.

Viewing the Flat Tops, one could easily believe it is a permanent fixture on the land. Yet, a close look reveals countless streams, draining countless hillsides. Each of these creeks removes tiny particles of rock, eroded by constant weathering. Before our eyes, the mountains that appear so solid are destroyed, a grain of sand at a time. This process of building mountain ranges and reducing them to rubble has occurred several times in this area. Let's review the processes that produced the Flat Tops' present shape.

The same events that have created the earth's present form were also at work in molding and sculpting the Flat Tops. It has long been speculated by scientists that the continents we now know were once united in a single land mass called Pangea. This single, massive continent began to break apart by a process called plate tectonics.

As the single, massive continent began to dissociate, the sea moved into the rifts that had been created. Several times, warm seas covered the lowlands east of the Flat Tops as Pangea crumbled.

The theory of plate tectonics suggests that continents, or plates, not only "drift" around over the earth's surface, moving apart, they also collide. When two plates crash together, the result is similar to that of two cars bumping — that is, if the collision takes place over eons rather than milliseconds. Fenders bend — sheet metal tears. Land compresses — rock shears.

Continents pushing against each other create tremendous stresses in the land. Compressional forces build mountains in a similar way a child might squeeze toy blocks together. The resulting forces fracture solid rock. Continued pressure moves some blocks of rock upward, some are shoved down.

Once blocks of rock are lifted, perhaps several thousand feet above sea level, nature goes to work tearing them down. Freezing and thawing cycles break apart solid rock. Rain and snow-melt removes eroded bits and pieces. Wind scatters small particles of sand. Over hundreds of millennia, once high mountains are worn down into nonexistence. Eroded sediment eventually comes to rest on the ocean floor. Mountains have arisen and fallen several times in the Flat Tops region.

Another phenomena controlled by plate tectonics is volcanism. Oceanic plates are denser than continental plates. On colliding, the oceanic plate moves beneath the continental plate. The denser rock moves deeper, contacting a zone of intense heat, melting the rock. As in a pot of boiling water, bubbles move upward from the bottom at the source of heat. The molten rock boils up, seeking escape. As it rises, continental crust is fractured, creating a path for the liquid magma to spew out and cover the land.

Eruptions away from the plate edges are usually mild, not violent as was Mount St. Helens for example. Basalt, a thick, black, molten rock coming from deep within the earth, flows and spreads out over the land in the same way chocolate frosting covers a layer cake. Mount Kilauea in Hawaii, while located on an ocean plate rather than a continent, is such a volcano. The volcanoes of the Flat Tops were similar in activity to Kilauea.

In the past twelve million years, ten or more mild eruptions spread basalt over the plateau. After spreading out over the surface, the basalt cooled, giving the Flat Tops its table-top appearance. Deep Lake, in the southeast quadrant of the area, was once a volcano on the Flat Tops.

Glaciers have also had a part in sculpting the area. During the most recent Ice Age, ending about ten thousand years ago, they worked on the many fractures in the uplift. Gorges were deepened. Deep Creek and the South Fork of the White River had their streambeds carved by glacial action. The thick sheet of ice carved the Chinese Wall near Trappers Lake.

Rubble was pushed ahead of the advancing ice wall. As the climate warmed and the glaciers melted, ridges of rock left behind formed dams, creating lakes here and there. Trappers Lake was likely dammed by glaciers.

The Ice Age ended a few thousand years ago. Volcanoes no longer pour out smoke and lava. However, the region has experienced geologic activity over the past ten millenia. Near the town of McCoy, an eruption occurred 8,000 years ago. Just over 4,000 years ago, about a mile north of Dotsero, occurred the most recent volcanic eruption in Colorado. The resulting lava flow dammed the Eagle River, creating a shallow lake. Through the ensuing centuries, the river slowly eroded the basalt barrier. The only remaining evidence of the pond you will find is the scattering of black boulders between Interstate 70 and the river, rock that once formed the low dam.

The forces that built the Flat Tops also created an ideal environment for life. The waters contain an abundance of life sustaining minerals for fish. The vegetation is rich in calcium, enabling elk to grow massive antlers. The land supports the largest deer and elk herds in the state. Wildflowers are abundant, both in quantity and variety.

While the construction of the Flat Tops has ended for now,

the area does not remain static. Nature acts continuously, remodeling, then destroying what she has built. It is rather like the ongoing highway construction projects. A look at the Colorado River in Glenwood Canyon confirms what we know. The river is never clear. It often appears as chocolate milk each spring, or after a summer thunderstorm, evidence that nature constantly erodes the land the river drains even as we watch.

The processes that gave us the Flat Tops and the Colorado Rockies also left valuable minerals in the state. Gold, deposited by hydrothermal solution in numerous locations throughout the state, attracted prospectors to Colorado hoping to strike it rich. The yellow metal, along with silver, molybdenum and other minerals contributed to Colorado's economy for more than a century. Several companies mine coal along the Yampa River drainage, east and north of the Flat Tops. However, with the exception of a small number of oil wells and minor placer gold deposits, the Flat Tops is nearly devoid of economic minerals.

With few resources to exploit, the area remained pristine. Few roads ever penetrated the wilderness on the Flat Tops. The sides are too steep. A short snow-free period of just four or five months and the high altitude make ranching impractical other than for summer grazing.

This high plateau has long been recognized as a place worth preserving. Old U.S. Forest Service maps show it as a primitive area, although Trappers Lake narrowly avoided development early in the century. Arthur H. Carhart, a landscape architect working for the Forest Service, convinced his supervisor Carl J. Stahl, that the lake shore should be preserved rather than developed for summer home sites. Carhart's dream later became a model for wilderness legislation. After years of debate, Congress passed the Wilderness Act of 1964. President Johnson signed it into law, preserving the Flat Tops. In 1978, Congress enlarged the boundaries, expanding the wilderness to its present size.

In the 4,000 years since the eruption at Dotsero Crater, little appears changed in the Flat Tops. A wilderness visitor today will enjoy the same magnificent vistas the Utes saw while hunting in the area a century and more ago. Elk still roam the area, sending their resonant mating calls echoing across the high glacial valleys each fall. Colorado River cutthroat, though threatened, still swim in their ancestral waters.

It is a place a person cannot visit just once. Visitors will be enticed to return, to explore a little further, to penetrate deeper into this untamed land.

Flora and Fauna

Colorado's largest deer and elk herds live in the area. In the ten years from 1983 through 1992, the elk herd nearly doubled in size, from an estimated 17,000 to nearly 30,000 animals. Deer numbers have stayed nearly constant, but they were plentiful to begin with. The White River herd, which covers the area from the Flat Tops to the Piceance Basin, is home to more than 80,000 deer.

Because of these high numbers, the Flat Tops is a popular hunting area. Hunter success rates on deer range from twenty to sixty percent, depending on the season and game unit. Elk hunters average from ten to forty percent success. Every year, trophy bulls are taken in the wilderness by a few lucky hunters.

While deer and elk are the most common big game, they're not the only large animals that live here. Though not common, bighorn sheep can be found. Bear and mountain lion also live in the wilderness. Because both are shy, you're not likely to see either.

Coyotes are widespread here as in other places in the west. You'll hear them serenading the moon most often at evening or dawn. The coyote's song makes a wilderness trip complete.

The Flat Tops is home for many small animals. You'll find cottontail rabbits and snowshoe hares. Porcupines are likely to appear anywhere. Your camp may be invaded by chipmunks at sometime. And pine squirrels will disturb the peace with their annoying, mindless chatter in the pine and spruce forest.

Field mice will be attracted to any tasty morsels you may have in your camp. These tiny tan creatures are most active after dark, when they feel safe from predators. Another small critter you find — you're likely to hear it rather than see it at first — resembles a mouse. You'll occasionally catch a glimpse of a vole running through tunnels in the grass and leaves. They're darker than mice and have very short tails.

The many high lakes and ponds are attractive to two furbearers; beaver and muskrat. Beaver become active at dusk as they begin swimming about the ponds. After dark, they work hard — well, they're busy as beavers — downing aspens to build and repair dams. Muskrats are much more casual about life. You may find these small, gray rodents at any time of day.

Birds are found on the Flat Tops in abundance. Song birds include robins, chickadees, Stellars, Gray jays, and warblers. Occasionally, you'll hear the deep croak of a passing raven. Woodpeckers include Hairys and Downys, as well as flickers. Should you plan to visit one of the many campgrounds, you may want to take a hummingbird feeder. Two species of hummingbird, the Broad-tail and Rufous, will be attracted to the nectar.

Redtail hawks are one of the more common birds of prey you'll see on the Flat Tops. With a bit of luck you may see a Peregrine falcon. You may also spot a Golden eagle soaring high above the plateau, using its incredible vision to sight a tiny meal.

Waterfowl also find the area attractive. Beaver ponds are often used by mallards and teal to raise families. Another game bird found on the Flat Tops is the Blue grouse. You'll find these birds on the edges of the area, close to timber.

The Flat Tops is an area containing large open meadows and immense stands of dense timber. The most common trees are spruce, fir, and lodgepole pines. These stands of timber also hold a great many snags — standing dead trees — in the wilderness. Back in the 1940s and 50s, an invasion of spruce beetles killed many trees. However, even after nearly 50 years, many are still standing, and represent a potential hazard in high wind.

Aspen groves are scattered all over the Flat Tops, especially at the lower elevations. They are a special attraction in the fall, when entire slopes appear as a solid yellow or gold. Willows grow profusely along streams and lakes, and sage is usually found on low elevation slopes.

Because of plentiful moisture, grasses are lush on the Flat Tops. Interspersed in the grasses is a multitude of wildflowers. Hidden among openings in the aspens, one can find columbines, the state flower.

Color varies with the season. July brings a variety of species and colors. Red, pink, white, blue, and yellow flowers often appear as a multicolored shag carpet. Blue flax, red elephants, lupines, and countless others decorate the wilderness. Fireweed — with its four-petaled pink blossoms — spring up along cuts and in bare areas. Paintbrush adds red to plain green weed patches in small openings in the timber. By August, yellows predominate. Daisies, sunflowers, and even dandelions color the hillsides. Throughout the summer, you'll find a variety of colors.

Climate

Because of its location, the Flat Tops receives an abundance of precipitation, making the region an anglers paradise. The plateau is the first obstacle any eastward-moving weather system encounters in this part of the state. The topography creates its own weather. Prevailing winds are from the west. Air moving from the west is forced to ascend in order to cross the wilderness, cooling in the process. Cooling condenses the water vapor, producing clouds that soon reach their dew point, bringing precipitation. This is a frequent year-round occurrence on the Flat Tops.

Winter snowfalls are abundant. Often, by early November, the plateau is inaccessible. The mantle of white rarely recedes before June or even July. Be aware, too, that snow can fall at any time of the year, even in summer.

Summer afternoon thundershowers are common. The day may begin with clear skies, but by noon, the first clouds form. Moments later, lightning flashes and thunder resounds across the plateau. The shower that follows may be brief but intense, or it can be a prelude to several days of rain.

While the region does receive more than its fair share of precipitation, summer also brings pleasantly warm, dry periods. Even at 11,000 feet, the days can be hot. During the summer, day time temperatures range from the 40s to the 80s while lows can vary from below freezing to the 50s.

Big game hunting begins with archery in late August and extends through Novermber. Though August and September are still summer on the calendar, the prudent hunter will prepare for the extremes. The first significant snow may fall in September, though it usually melts in a few days. Jack Frost makes his first appearance then, too, bringing the first fall color to the high county.

October is frequently accompanied by a lull in weather patterns. Deer and elk hunters often find the days balmy in spite of night time freezes. Nevertheless it's still wise to prepare for severe conditions. Late in the month, the season has progressed enough that snow begins accumulating. Shorter days and cooler temperatures mean less melting. Soon, the plateau will be covered in white, inaccessible until the following summer.

The wilderness is closed half the year to all but snowshoers and cross-county skiers. And while high lakes begin to open in May, most trails are still drifted shut. A trip to one of the early-opening lakes will require skis or snowshoes. As a general guideline, areas below 9,000 feet should be accessible by Memorial Day. In June, plan your trips to locations below 10,000 feet and by July, the entire wilderness should be open though you may find scattered snow drifts. Of course, all this is dependent on the winter snowfall and exposure. South facing areas tend to open first. In dry years, the wilderness may open earlier.

Access

Interstate 70 runs east-west across Colorado. It is the primary access route to the Flat Tops from Denver, east of the Rockies, and Grand Junction to the west, thirty miles from the Utah line. The road follows the Colorado River along the south side of the White River Plateau.

State Highway 13 runs north from Interstate 70 at the town of Rifle. This two-lane paved road takes you along the Grand Hogback on the west flank of the plateau to the town of Meeker, forty-one miles from Rifle. Continuing along this route, State 13 reaches Craig, situated on Highway 40, some forty-eight miles north of Meeker. U.S. Highway 40, while it doesn't traverse the plateau, does give access to the Flat Tops from the north.

From Steamboat Springs, forty-two miles east of Craig at the west side of Rabbit Ears Pass, State Highway 131 goes south to join Interstate 70 at Wolcott. It passes through the communities of Oak Creek, Phippsburg, Toponas, and Yampa, each of which gives access to the eastern areas of the Flat Tops.

Kremmling, a small ranching community on U.S. 40, lies fifty-two miles east of Steamboat Springs and 112 miles west of Denver. It doesn't give access to the Flat Tops but six miles west of town, State Highway 134 crosses Gore Pass to connect with State Highway 131 at Toponas.

In addition to the major state and federal all-weather roads, there is a network of county roads accessing the Flat Tops Wilderness. From New Castle, halfway between Glenwood Springs and Rifle on Interstate 70, a gravel road, the New Castle — Buford Road, takes you north to Buford. In the White River National Forest, it's Forest Road 244 and in Rio Blanco County, it becomes County Road 17.

Rio Blanco County Road 8 heads east from Meeker and takes you into the north side of the wilderness at several points. Between Meeker and the Lost Creek Guard Station east of Buford, the road is paved for a distance of about twenty-five miles. The road takes you over Ripple Creek Pass and on to the towns of Oak Creek, Phippsburg, and Yampa, another 40 miles to the east. From Yampa, Routt County Road 7 on the south side of town leads west for seventeen miles to Stillwater Reservoir over narrow, rough pavement that changes to gravel at the forest boundary.

Eagle County Road 301, a good gravel road, follows the Colorado River. This road takes off from State Highway 131 near the community of McCoy and provides access to the Derby, Sweetwater, and Deep Creek Roads.

Forest Road 600 leaves Eagle County Road 301 at the Colorado River 1.5 miles north of Interstate 70. This road gives the only access to the south side of the Flat Tops Wilderness, thirty-nine miles from the blacktop.

Road access is dependent both on maintenance and season. Federal and state highways are maintained in all weather conditions. County roads are cleared where year round access is needed. Roads that are usually, but not always opened by Memorial Day are

Rio Blanco County Road 8 over Ripple Creek Pass, Routt County Road 7 to Stillwater Reservoir, and Garfield County Road 150 up Sweetwater Creek. Forest Road 600, on the plateau leading to the southeast part of the wilderness, is usually open by July 4, sometimes earlier. It's best to check with the White River National Forest supervisor at Glenwood Springs, (303) 945-2521, before making travel plans.

Chapter Two

Regulations and Common Sense

The freedom to travel wherever we like, includes a responsibility. Most of us care about a quality wilderness experience. It's the few who don't care that make regulations necessary. Fortunately, most are common sense practices that will make your Flat Tops visit more enjoyable. Flat Tops Wilderness regulations are available from Forest Service offices in Glenwood Springs, Eagle, Rifle, Meeker, and Yampa, and are posted at all trailheads.

Regulations

1. Locate campsites, campfires, and recreational stock at least 100 feet from lakes, steams, and trails. At Hooper, Keener, Trappers, and Smith lakes, locate camps at least 1/4 mile from the lake shore. Camping is allowed only in designated sites at Deer Lake. Vegetation and soils adjacent to lakes and streams are sensitive to disturbance. Camping away from trails and lakes adds to visitors sense of solitude.

2. The largest party size is a combination of 25 people and/ or recreational stock. Larger groups tend to damage trails and campsites.

3. Use of motorized vehicles, motorized equipment, motor boats, or other forms of mechanical transport such as bicycles, handcarts, etc., within the wilderness is prohibited.

4. Landing of aircraft or dropping of materials, supplies, or persons from aircraft in the wilderness is prohibited.

5. Camping, campfires, and hitching or tethering of recreational stock is prohibited within 1/4 mile of Trappers Lake. Dogs, except for working stock dogs, accompanying a blind person, and dogs used for legal hunting purposes will be on a leash not to exceed six feet in length when within 1/4 mile of Trappers Lake.

6. Pets must be under control at all times. Uncontrolled dogs harass wildlife and other visitors.

7. For livestock, bring in only processed feeds or pellets. Hay may introduce noxious weeds and exotic plants to the wilderness.

8. Equipment, personal property, or supplies may not be left for more than 14 continuous days.

No Trace Camping

While not a written law, wilderness visitors are encouraged to practice no trace camping. A free booklet, LEAVE NO TRACE! An Outdoor Ethic, is available at Forest Service district offices. Here are a few suggestions from the Forest Service.

1. Select camp areas well away from lakes and steams. Your camp should not be visible from the trail so others can experience solitude. Most impact occurs around lakes. To avoid other groups of campers, mud, and insects, select a meadow camp site.

2. Use pack stoves, especially in areas of heavy use. If a campfire is necessary, make a small pit fire. Do not build rock fire rings. Rocks and soil are easily scarred by a fire. Erase all signs of fire when you leave.

3. Wash at least 100 feet from lakes and streams. Use biodegradable soap and dispose of waste water in the soil.

4. Bury human waste at least 100 feet from lakes and streams and six inches in the soil so it will decompose naturally.

5. Pack out everything you bring in and any other trash you may find along the way. Food scraps and bits of paper may be burned. Do not bury trash or food scraps.

6. Pets should be on a leash or under control and attended by their owner. Don't permit them to disturb wildlife.

7. Travel in small groups to avoid major impact on the land.

8. Avoid the use of brightly colored or fluorescent clothing, packs, and tents to reduce visual impact. The only exception to this is during rifle-hunting seasons when hunters are required to wear blaze-orange.

9. When hiking cross-county, that is, off trails, spread out the group to avoid creating new paths.

10. Radios and tape players don't belong in the back country. Keep noise levels down on trails and in camp.

Avoid fragile areas. Do not short-cut trails on switchbacks, especially in places others might follow and create new paths that lead to erosion. Rarely will the practice save any time.

You are requested to fill out a wilderness permit to assist USFS personnel in managing the wilderness. It will also help rangers to locate you in case of emergency. Permits can be obtained at all trailheads leading into the wilderness.

On the subject of permits, lodges and outfitters usually have small areas reserved for their use as camp sites. These areas may be used *only* by the outfitters, their employees, and clients. These sites will be identified by a Forest Service permit near the camp.

Pack animals are a part of the wilderness experience for some visitors. Hikers and backpackers meeting riders and pack animals should step off the trail until they pass. If you take Phydeaux, restrain him until horses have passed to avoid spooking them.

Remember that wildflowers are for viewing and not picking.

There's no need to dig a trench around any modern, good quality backpacking tent. It's also unsightly and leads to erosion of the volcanic clay soils that predominate here.

In some cases, the use of wheelchairs may be permitted by the disabled. Check with the Forest Service first, though.

No matter where we go, there's one thing that will always be found; trash. There is no excuse for leaving litter. Most camping garbage can be burned. Aluminum beverage cans should be crushed, then packed out. After all, they weighed almost a pound when you took them in full and almost nothing when you take them out empty. If you can't pack your trash, stay out of the Flat Tops.

While they may not be trash, meat poles put up by hunters detract from the visual experience in the wilderness. If you need one, build it using rope rather than bailing wire, which cuts into trees, then dismantle it when you pack out your game. Fluorescent flagging to mark downed game is also unsightly. If you must use flagging, remove it when it's no longer needed. Many hunters use horses in the Flat Tops. Rather than build corrals to contain stock, use the low impact methods suggested in *Horse Sense*, available free from the Forest Service.

The most important rule to remember in the wilderness is to respect the land. Practicing low impact travel preserves the land for future generations. Treat the Flat Tops as if you owned it. The wilderness is YOUR land. Respect it.

The Flat Tops has a lot of snags caused by disease and insects years ago. For this reason, especially careful with fires, whether using wood or a stove. Keep your campfire small. Use only dead wood. Also, select a camp site away from snags. The USFS estimates that ten snags per acre are felled by wind each year.

Douse your fire anytime you leave camp. Should your unattended fire spread, you can be held financially responsible for the expense of fighting it.

Leave no trace after you break camp. Dig a small pit for your fire, saving the soil. When you leave, replace the sod. Sweep the area you tracked with your lug-soled boots, using natural materials. Do the same to matted down vegetation. In a short time, your campsite will appear to have never been used.

Emergencies

Animals

While bears, lions, coyotes, and other carnivores live in the Flat Tops, you're unlikely to have problems with any of them. Chipmunks that steal your gorp and gray jays that beg handouts are normally the extent of predation experienced by visitors. However that doesn't mean you shouldn't use caution.

The Colorado Division of Wildlife publishes several free pamphlets concerning dangerous animals.

Bears are the most feared because of their size, and the fact that they eat whatever they want. Most will try to avoid you. Since bears are always hungry, food smells can attract them. The use of commercial freeze-dried foods kept in original packages will reduce the odor problem.

Don't eat or store food in your tent. Burn trash and food scraps. Keep you campsite clean.

If you see a bear on the trail, make noise. Don't approach it. If the animal comes toward you, don't turn and run. Instead, slowly back away until you are in a safer position. Try to get upwind so the bear can catch your scent.

Should you carry bear repellant, that is, a .357 or .44 Magnum? Chances are you'll never need a gun for protection from bears or other wild animals in the wilderness.

Should you see a mountain lion, consider yourself lucky. In three decades of living in and travelling through the back country, the closest I have come to a big cat is finding tracks. So, if you should be so fortunate, how do you react? First of all, don't run. This will induce a cat to attack. Face the animal but avoid eye contact, which the cat perceives as a threat. Raise your arms to appear larger. Speak softly to the animal and begin backing away.

Other carnivores you'll possibly see in the Flat Tops pose little threat. Bobcats are secretive, and if seen at all they're usually running away. Coyotes avoid humans. They've had too many unpleasant experiences around man.

Environmental Hazards

Hypothermia

No matter what season you visit the Flat tops, hypothermia is possible. In winter, the obvious contributor is cold and snow, but the hazard also exists in summer.

Because the Flat Tops get rain frequently, and the high elevation causes lower temperatures, you should stay dry. Modern rain gear makes this possible.

The problem is not just the dampness but the chill it produces. Relative humidity at high elevations is usually low, causing rapid evaporation. An air temperature of 50 degrees combined with a 10 m.p.h. wind, can give the same cooling effect as a temperature in the 40s. If your clothes have been soaked by a sudden shower, the evaporation causes even more cooling. Most cases of hypothermia occur at temperatures between 30 and 50.

Hypothermia will cause severe shivering, slurred speech, incoherence, stumbling, drowsiness, and extreme fatigue. If you do get wet and notice any of these symptoms in yourself or someone with you, immediate treatment is advised.

Get out of the wind. Remove all wet clothes. Put on dry clothes and crawl into a sleeping bag. The victim should be given warm drinks if he/she is coherent and able to swallow. It may be necessary to use your body heat to warm a hypothermic person.

Lightning

Thunder storms occur frequently in the Flat Tops. So does lightning. The plateau has several large clear areas, free of trees. Be cautious about hiking in the open anytime storms are threatening. If electrical storms are a possibility, stay close to shelter. During an electrical storm, avoid open areas or lone trees.

If you are caught in the open, remove your pack, which likely contains conductive metal. Squat down with your feet together. Imitate a ball with your body. In this position, a lightning strike should pass over your body in what's called a "flashover." If you're hiking in a group, spread apart to reduce the chance of a strike hitting the entire party.

Forest Fire

Get out of the area and don't hang around to watch it. Report fires to the nearest USFS district office.

Other Hazards

The Flat Tops has lots of standing dead trees. Select a campsite with this in mind. Strong winds, common in the Flat Tops, are all it takes to knock one down.

Get your water only from known safe sources, or treat it before drinking. Assume that any surface water is contaminated.

Water can be filtered, boiled, or chemically treated to kill giardia. Using only water that has been processed with barley and hops will also eliminate such problems. Oh. While a beer may taste good after hiking all day, be aware that alcohol gains potency at high altitude, and can also contribute to dehydration, a cause of altitude illness.

Insects are abundant on the Flat Tops. Bring repellant. Lots. Garlic is also said to repel mosquitoes. Presumably, if you eat sufficient quantities of this delicious seasoning — enough that your friends keep their distance — insects won't hang around you, either.

Snakes are not a serious problem. Most of those you see are garter snakes. You might even come across an occasional bull snake. Although generally harmless, bull snakes can grow to substantial size and sometimes act threateningly. They will bite if provoked. However their bite is not poisonous though tetanus could result and it's always a good idea to be immunized against tetanus. Timber rattlesnakes could live in the Flat Tops but if they do, they're rare.

Livestock

Horses are not the only livestock you will encounter on the Flat Tops. You will also meet up with cattle and sheep.

Usually, cows will run from you. But not always. A cow with a calf is protective of her offspring. If she sees you as a threat, she will get belligerent, especially, after being on the range all summer.

Bulls also present a problem. When cows are in heat, a bull has only one thing on his mind. A bull having amorous thoughts is an animal to avoid. If you're not a cow, he will see you as an object on which to express his aggression. Avoid bulls, even if you must go out of your way.

Sheep are also grazed in the wilderness, most often in the high meadows. Grazing is a historical use of the forests and was grandfathered into wilderness laws. You can reduce the probability of contacting livestock by inquiring at the appropriate district office to learn areas where sheep or cattle are being grazed.

There's one other hazard, but you are the only person who can prevent it. That's carelessness. Read the signs posted at trailheads. They inform you of wilderness regulations that protect both you and the resource, You don't need to go to the extremes that would be required by OSHA if they were to regulate wilderness travel but prudence is required. You go to the Flat Tops to enjoy the experience. Don't ruin it by doing something dumb. The wilderness is unforgiving of mistakes.

Altitude Illness: Don't Let It Get You Down

Anyone who visits the Flat Tops, whether you live in Colorado or the Gulf coast, is a potential victim of altitude illness. A recent study found one in four visitors to a mountain resort had some altitude related symptoms.

"Far too many serious incidents occur during mountain outings because the participants are unaware of the debilitating effects of dehydration and high altitudes," says Chief Master Sergeant Peter Kummerfeldt, SERE (Survival Evasion Resistance Escape) instructor at the U.S. Air Force Academy, hunter, and high altitude expert. Dr. Tom Morgan, a Colorado Springs physician practicing in the field of high altitude sports medicine, agrees.

What causes a person to have physical problems at high altitude? According to Dr. Morgan, it has to do with air pressure. The decrease in pressure that comes with an increase in altitude reduces the quantity of oxygen available. At sea level, your blood is 100 percent saturated with oxygen. When we venture into high altitudes, the reduced air pressure reduces oxygen saturation. We adapt to the oxygen deficiency by breathing faster and deeper, and increasing cardiovascular output.

Physical problems with altitude vary but can be grouped into three separate though related forms: Acute mountain sickness or AMS, high altitude pulmonary edema, or fluid in the lungs and high altitude cerebral edema, fluid on the brain. They are commonly abbreviated HAPE and HACE.

AMS is rarely seen below 6500 feet. However, it becomes increasingly common above 8,000 feet, an elevation easily reached on the Flat Tops. Symptoms are usually minor though they can be disabling. Severity is greater among those who haven't taken time for acclimatization. A person making a rapid ascent may experience a headache — mild to severe — nausea, vomiting, shortness of breath, weakness, sleep disturbance, or experience periods of irregular breathing.

Left untreated, AMS can advance to a serious, life-threatening illness, HAPE. It most often effects those who have had the problem previously, or have been acclimatized to high altitude, spent two or more weeks at low elevations, and then returned to the higher altitude. The symptoms can develop rather rapidly, sometimes in a matter of hours, or slowly over a period of one to three days. HAPE is not always accompanied by symptoms of AMS.

A person suffering from HAPE will experience shortness of breath, irritating cough, weakness, rapid heart rate, and headache. The problem frequently worsens at night. A pulse rate higher than 110 per minute and respiration in excess of 16 breaths per minute

27

is an early sign of HAPE. A medical emergency exists should the rates exceed 120 and 20. If the illness is untreated, the victim can go into a coma. Death may follow within a very short time.

A person suffering from HAPE must immediately be evacuated to lower altitude, preferably below 6500 feet. Oxygen may help mild cases but descent is still necessary. When a Gamow Bag (Gam — off) is available, it should be used. This inflatable device simulates descent. Recovery after descent, whether actual or simulated in the Gamow Bag, is usually rapid.

HACE is less common than the other forms of altitude illness but is the most severe. Symptoms include severe headache, confusion, hallucinations, unstable gait, loss of vision, loss of dexterity, and facial muscle paralysis. A sufferer may fall into a restless sleep, followed by deep coma and death. Immediate descent or use of the Gamow Bag is required if the victim is to have any hope of recovery. Oxygen, if available, should be given by face mask at the rate of 2-4 liters per minute.

Symptoms of all three forms of altitude illness are progressive. Some are overlapping. It doesn't follow, however, that one form will always progress to another, more serious condition. A person can have HAPE or HACE without first showing symptoms of AMS.

Anyone showing signs of HAPE or HACE should be taken to lower altitude immediately. On the north side of the Flat Tops, the nearest medical facility is at Meeker. If you exit the wilderness by I-70, treatment is available at Glenwood Springs.

A person might think that a physical conditioning program would prevent altitude illness. It ain't so. Fitness will give you more endurance and aid in the efficient use of oxygen, but it won't prevent altitude problems. Even if your fitness level is excellent, don't let it lull you into overextending yourself before acclimatization.

A conditioning program should begin at least twelve weeks prior to traveling to high altitude. The body requires this long to respond to physical training. And remember that acclimatization is lost once a person has returned to low altitude (below 6500 feet) after as little as ten days.

Even after completing a conditioning program, a person who lives near sea level is going to require time to acclimate to high altitude. When possible, you should allow two or three days to adjust to the altitude before engaging in any rigorous activity after arrival. Even then, you'll likely feel more tired than usual from normal activities.

Smoking will decrease your performance at altitude and should be avoided.

Those who suffer from respiratory ailments such as asthma should be aware that these conditions can be aggravated by high altitude if not treated. Other ailments such as pulmonary hypertension may also be aggrivated. Anyone who uses medications for these conditions must also use them at altitude. One caution, though; The use of sedating antihistamines (the kind that make you drowsy) can decrease respiration while sleeping, worsening some symptoms of altitude illness.

Both Chief Kummerfeldt and Dr. Morgan agree that dehydration contributes to altitude sickness. Under ordinary conditions, the body needs two to four quarts of water per day to stay hydrated. At altitudes above 8000 feet, fluid requirements increase. Three or four quarts per day should be considered a minimum. Thirst is a poor indicator of need. Get lots of fluids and drink frequently. Avoid, or at least minimize the use of beverages containing caffeine or alcohol as these contribute to dehydration.

Electrolyte replacement drinks are assimilated quickly. Those in powder form can be carried easily and mixed with water, ready for use as needed. Just make certain you get adequate fluids, whichever type you use. As long as your urine is colorless or very light yellow, you are sufficiently hydrated.

While diet won't prevent altitude sickness, certain foods are recommended because they are easier to digest. Meals high in complex carbohydrates such as pastas, breads, or whole grain cereals are good energy sources. The body tends to run out of steam easier at high altitude. Carbohydrates help offset this effect. Proteins and fats should be used in moderation since they are difficult to metabolize.

Some people are more susceptible to altitude illness than others. Medical help is available for this situation. Dr. Paul Auerbach, Chief, Division of Emergency Medicine at the Stanford University Hospital, recommends the use of *Diamox* (acetazolomide) to aid acclimatization. 125-250 mg, taken twice daily, is advised, beginning 6-12 hours before ascent and continued for 24-48 hours after reaching the maximum altitude. It should be included in the medical kit for altitudes over 9000 feet. A prescription is required.

Diamox does have some side effects. It will cause increased urination so get more fluids to prevent dehydration. It can also cause tingling in your fingers and toes shortly after taking each dose. Taking the smaller dosage will reduce the frequency of urination. The tingling sensation shouldn't last very long. The symptoms, while annoying, are less so than altitude illness. One word of caution, though: Don't take this medication if you are allergic to sulfa drugs.

Decadron (dexamethasone), an anti-inflammatory steroid, is useful for treating symptoms of AMS until the victim can be taken to lower altitude. This is also a prescription drug. Either of these medications, *Decadron* or *Diamox*, **should be used only as directed by a physician.**

Minor headaches associated with AMS can be relieved with ordinary over-the counter-pain medications such as aspirin, acetaminophen, or ibuprofen. If you're having headaches, however, you may not be getting enough water. To prevent further difficulty, do not ascend to higher altitude until you are free of a headache for 12 hours.

The best way a person can prepare for a high altitude adventure is to spend a lot of time at that altitude. For the majority of us, this isn't practical. The next best thing is to prepare physically and mentally. Understanding acclimatization and getting yourself in top physical condition will improve your ability to meet the challenge of the Flat Tops.

Chapter Three

Getting The Most From Your Maps

Mountain man Jim Bridger was once asked if he ever got lost while wandering the uncharted west of the 1830s. His carefully considered reply was "Well, I ain't never been lost but I was a might confused once for a month or two."

Bridger didn't have the many advantages we enjoy today. The U.S. Geological Survey (USGS) has mapped the entire country in 7.5 minute topographic quadrangles. Fine detail makes it possible to know the land you plan to hike before visiting the area.

A topographic (usually referred to as a topo) map tells the user about terrain, vegetation, trails, roads, water, and many other natural and man made surface features. A topo is indispensable in planning a trail adventure.

The topo is your primary means of navigating the Flat Tops (or any other wilderness.) It is the only type of map having sufficient detail to pinpoint your location. When used with a compass, you should be able to find your location within a few hundred feet. That's not as precise as the Global Positioning System using satellite telemetry, but it's good enough for backcountry travel.

If you're not familiar with the maps, pick up a copy of *Topographic Maps*, free from USGS. It tells you what is needed to read a topo. In addition, it discusses map making, mapping sources and accuracy standards, and the various types published. One section explains the map symbols.

The most important symbol is the continuous brown contour line that indicates elevation. Even if the other symbols aren't understood, the contour line is probably familiar. Always printed in brown, it represents the form seen from the air above the ground if a horizontal slice were removed from the earth at that elevation. Contour lines far apart indicate the land is sort of flat. When they're close together, it means the ground is steep. A trail crossing close contours means a hiker will sweat and puff hard after a short ascent. The trail, of course, is the dashed black line that somehow is always located in the steepest terrain.

Each contour line represents a fixed vertical interval, stated at the bottom of the map. Moving from one brown line to the next means a change in elevation as indicated by the interval.

Contours tell the user much about the terrain. Remember the rule of Vs. A contour forms a V when crossing a stream and the closed end points upstream. If the V is relatively long, with several contour lines close together, the stream is in a canyon. If the points of several Vs are close together, expect to find rapids or falls on the stream.

Water features, lakes, streams, reservoirs, and ponds, are shown in blue. A solid blue line indicates a stream, river, or creek that runs year round. If the line is interrupted with a series of three dots, the stream usually runs only part of the year, like after runoff.

One important symbol appears at the lower left corner of a topo; the magnetic declination. The angle between True North and Magnetic North varies depending on your geographic location. This angle must be accounted for when taking a compass bearing on a landmark. Even though it's only about 12 degrees on the Flat Tops, failing to account for it can produce an error in locating your position when distant landmarks are used. Uncorrected, deviation can produce an error of a half-mile if you are using landmarks five miles away. When possible, sight on nearby landmarks to more precisely locate your position.

To locate your position on the topo, first turn it so it's oriented, that is, the top of the map points north. Pick out three features on the map you can identify on the ground. Each should be about 120 degrees apart. With your compass, sight on the first landmark. Note the bearing, or direction in degrees. Next, mark the bearing on the map through your landmark and your approximate position using the straightedge of the compass. Repeat this for each feature. When you've finished, the three lines form a small triangle. Your position should be near the center of the triangle.

In addition to topos, the wilderness hiker will find other useful maps. U.S. Forest Service (USFS) and Bureau of Land Management (BLM) maps show the surface ownership of the land. This information is especially important to recreationists to avoid unintentionally trespassing on private land.

But why would a person need to use other types of maps with a topo? There are several reasons.

Take a look at a USFS map. It has no details such as that found on a topo. It does, however, have information not found on the USGS quads. A USFS map shows the boundaries of each national forest. Trails and roads are numbered. Like BLM maps they show the ownership of land in the area covered. To some, it may be a surprise to find private land inside the boundary of a forest. A hiker will be trespassing there just as he would if walking through a city yard, or agricultural land on the plains.

On both the USFS and BLM maps, colors are used to code ownership status. Green indicates Forest Service lands, yellow or salmon marks BLM land, while blue denotes state, and white means private land.

One important bit of information to keep in mind about maps. As good as are those published by USGS, BLM and USFS, you will still find areas on maps that disagree. This problem is caused by the frequency of updates by the various mapping agencies.

USGS quads covering the Flat Tops Wilderness were completed in 1966 and 1977, with one 1966 quad being photo-revised in 1987. The newest quad is nearly ten years old. While the topography won't change, other features will. Roads shown on older topos may now be closed, and new trails appear on the ground.

The latest USFS map of the White River National Forest was completed in 1991. BLM published an updated map of the region in late 1993. These maps however, do not show topography, which means you must use several maps together in order to have a current picture of surface features and the latest road and trail data.

Trails Illustrated, a map company in Evergreen, CO has solved this problem. They publish maps of the more popular recreational areas of Colorado, using the USGS quads as a base. Data from many sources is incorporated to make a map having the topography, driveable roads, current trails, and surface ownership. The maps are field checked and updated every two or three years to keep them current. Each Trails Illustrated map incorporates eight to twelve USGS quads and is printed on durable plastic at a cost about one-fourth that of the Survey quads covering the same area. The scale is 1:40,000 making a conveniently-sized, weather-resistant map that fits your pocket.

In addition to the maps published by federal and state agencies, there are others that will be of value to the outdoor adventurer.

What's the best way to carry a map on a hike or backpack trip? USGS quads measure about 22 by 27 inches so they must be folded for convenience. However, folding and unfolding causes wear and tear, and moisture causes the paper to deteriorate.

The Aquaseal people make a product called "Mapseal" that make maps more durable. It's a waterproofing liquid you brush on your maps. Paper treated with this will be water repellant and less likely to tear along the folds. In addition to this treatment, you should also carry your maps in a heavy-duty Ziplock® or similar locking plastic bag.

The wilderness traveller has never had it better than we do today. Maps are made that show surface details, roads and hiking trails, or places to fish and hunt. Land ownership status informs you of places to enjoy without worrying about trespassing illegally. If Ol' Jim had carried one of the maps we have available, his confusion would have been of much shorter duration.

Hiking The Flat Tops Wilderness

Because the Flat Tops Wilderness is large, it's a great place to get away from it all, on foot or horseback. Whether you plan a day hike or an extended backpack trip, you'll be able to find a trail that offers the experience you seek.

First of all, keep in mind that whichever trail you take, expect an ascent. With few exceptions, count on climbing at least a thousand feet to reach the plateau. Indeed, one trail, number 1825, ascends nearly four thousand feet.

Once you're on top, though, the hike or horse ride is easy. The plateau is nearly flat and in some areas, you can hike several miles with no significant change in elevation, although be advised that doesn't mean it's absolutely level. If you're following the maps reproduced in this guide or a topo map, be aware of the contour interval. It's forty feet, and as one hiker said, it can hide a lot of thirty nine-foot anomalies.

If you've never used one, take a hiking staff. You'll be pleasantly surprised at the stability it gives when carrying a loaded backpack on rough, uneven terrain. Trails in the Flat Tops are usually pretty good, but in many places, cobbles and occasional boulders litter the trails. You will also appreciate a staff on steep trails. Using one can help you avoid a fall should you stumble on a rough section of the trail.

What length hiking staff should you select? One that's shoulder-high should be about right. If you're cheap and don't care to purchase a factory-made model, select a solid dead stick. Use your knife to trim the rough spots so it won't rub blisters on you hands.

What should a hiker wear on the Flat Tops? That all depends on the season of course, but in the summer, shorts and t-shirts work fine while walking. Nights on the plateau can get cool. If you live in the lowlands, it probably will seem cold. Carry long pants and a jacket for evenings in camp and a water-repellant parka and pants for rain. A baseball cap or "boonie" hat will protect your head from the sun and sunburn. Use sunscreen on exposed skin. The sun burns faster at high altitude.

Good sturdy boots are essential to enjoying your Flat Tops hike. You don't need heavy-duty climbing boots, but you will need good support for carrying a heavy pack. Some of the new lightweight model boots should work fine here as long as they aren't sloppy, and provide good traction on wet clay soils. Gore Tex® will help keep your feet dry while crossing shallow streams and in the showers that occur frequently on the Flat Tops. Good water-resistant boots also allow you to practice low-impact hiking. John Anarella, a Wilderness Ranger for the Yampa District, says you should go ahead and slop through the mud on the trail. Walking on the trailside vegetation to keep dry contributes to erosion of the path.

Pilgrims And Horses

Backpacking isn't the only way to see the Flat Tops. A physical problem may make it difficult for some to walk the long distances necessary. Hunters usually need more gear than can easily be carried on their backs over long distances. Packing game, especially elk, is done quickly with horses. Other visitors may want to enjoy a total Western experience. For these people, a horse pack trip is as important as seeing the wilderness itself. A dozen or more resorts and outfitters offer such trips in the Flat tops.

Horses and dudes are sometimes a disaster waiting to happen. Under the best of circumstances, horses can be unpredictable. Colorado recognizes the inherent danger and has passed laws relieving an outfitter of responsibility for accidents with riding and pack stock, even in cases resulting in death. Therefore, it is incumbent on the rider to learn basic horsemanship, riding technique, horse etiquette, and rider-horse communication.

Knowledge of basic horsemanship will yield two benefits; it will reduce the probability of an accident, and it will add pleasure to a unique outdoor experience.

Get to know your horse. As with humans, horses are individuals. Each has its own special personality. Some are affectionate and enjoy having their muzzles stroked. Others have a sense of humor. You'll find lazy horses that lag behind at a slow pace, then suddenly break into a trot when they fall too far behind. Fortunately, few are mean. Responsible outfitters cull such critters from their riding stock.

While the wrangler is saddling the horses, get acquainted with the one you will ride. Talk to him as you stroke his nose and scratch his cheek. Remember, though, that you should never approach a horse from behind unless you make him aware of you presence. Communicate by touching. Rub his neck. Give him a pat. As you move around behind, keep your hand on his hindquarters so the horse knows where you are and that you are not a threat he should kick.

From the saddle, the ground looks far away. What do I do now, you think. Relax. Yes, it's easy to say and hard to practice. Most saddle horses owned by outfitters are gentle, but problems can arise when the animal detects your apprehension. As soon as you're in the saddle, the horse knows what kind of rider you are and what he can get away with. Be friendly, but at the same time, show confidence. This will let him know you're in control.

The traditional way to mount is from the horse's left side. Hold the reins in your left hand and shorten them to make light contact with the horse's mouth. Face the horse and place your left foot in the stirrup. Your left hand should be on the horse's neck, your right on the cantle, or back of the saddle. Lift yourself by straightening your left leg. Avoid pulling yourself up as this will unbalance the animal.

Once you are up, bring your right leg across the hindquarters, keeping your leg straight. While show form isn't important here, avoid contacting the horse with your right leg as you swing it over. Sit in the saddle and place your right foot in the stirrup.

Dismounting is done in reverse order with one difference. After swinging your right leg around, support your weight with your hands on the saddle, slide the left foot out of the stirrup and lower yourself to the ground.

Mounting and dismounting should always be done with horse and rider facing the same direction to prevent the danger of catching a foot in the stirrup should the horse move. If the horse should bolt, your foot will easily come out of the untwisted stirrup. Keep in mind that in some situations, you will want to get on or off the horse from the opposite, or right side.

The first thing the wrangler should do, even before unhitching the horse, is check and adjust the stirrup length. The usual way is to set the length so that you have a couple of inches between your crotch and the saddle when you stand in the stirrups. An alternate method is to adjust the stirrup so that the bottom is at your ankle. This will give the correct clearance when you stand. With your feet in the stirrups, your toes will be angled slightly upward. This will stretch your calf muscles and can cause soreness on a long ride. Stretching exercises will reduce this problem.

Once in the saddle, you should now recall your mother's words as she told you to "sit up straight." With the horse on level ground, your position should be as if standing with your knees bent slightly and pitched forward.

Now, everyone is ready to hit the trail. Your horse, however, has decided to stay. Tell him to go as you gently squeeze your heels into his sides. This action and the fact that he sees his buddies leaving will encourage him to get in gear.

One thing you must do from the beginning is establish who is boss. The reins are used to communicate your commands to the horse. At the same time, you must be gentle. Only slight back pressure is needed to tell the horse to "whoa." The bit in the horse's mouth lets you control him. It requires only slight movement to cause pain. Don't jerk back hard on the reins. You'll only succeed in making him want to get rid of you. Confidence in yourself is the best way to establish yourself as master. Talking to the animal in a pleasant tone is also helpful.

One of the first things your horse will try is the "munch test." As you ride along, he'll suddenly reach down to bite off a clump of grass, almost pulling the reins from your grip. If you allow it once the horse has won. Hold the reins firmly so when the pulls, he'll feel the bit, discouraging him from grazing at the wrong time.

Some horses are laggards and would rather take it easy. You may find yourself falling behind the others. Suddenly, it seems, your horse notices he's being left and wants to catch up. What do you do when he starts running?

Though it may seem as though your horse is running at high speed, he isn't But you're being bounced around and each time your crotch hits the seat, it hurts. Relax. Stand in the stirrups and lean forward. If it makes you feel better, grip the horn. In a few seconds, you'll catch up to the others and the pace will be easier.

There will be occasions when your saddle slips to one side or the other. Again, remember your mother's reprimand. If the cinch is properly tightened, and you sit upright in the saddle, with your weight over the horse's back, this won't happen. With proper technique, you should be able to mount a horse with no cinch on the saddle. If it's slipping, you're causing it by not sitting centered over the horse.

Each horse will approach an obstacle differently. This is where you must pay attention to how he will react to, say a log across the path. Some horses prefer jumping over waist-high downed trees to stepping over or going around these obstacles. If the horse hesitates while tight against a log, is tensed with his legs gathered, be prepared to jump. Lean your upper body forward to stay balanced. Although it's not proper form, inexperienced riders may also want to grip the mane with the free hand.

Your horse will let you know what he's thinking or planning if you take time to notice. Watch his ears and head. If the animal is looking intently at something, his ears attentive or laid back, he may be ready to spook. When he does, anything can happen. Calm the animal by speaking gently to give assurance. Once he's at ease and knows you're in control, he should respond to you rather than the thing that caused apprehension.

There's a lot more you can learn about horses and riding, but this should help you feel comfortable on a horse. Any good book store should have a few titles you'll want to read. Visit a riding stable before you go off on a pack trip. The more you learn and ride, the greater your enjoyment will be when riding the Flat Tops.

Chapter Four
A word about the trail descriptions in this book

The trails are grouped by road access. Descriptions begin at Meeker, at the northwest corner of the Flat Tops, and go clockwise around the Wilderness Area.

The description gives a brief synopsis of the trail. The destination tells what you'll find along the way and at the end of the trail. Distances given for trails are approximate. Time required for hiking a trail is not included as there are too many variables for an estimate to have meaning.

Elevations are given for the trailhead and trailend. In some cases, neither point is the high or low elevation for the trail so this is also included when it occurs somewhere else on the trail.

Directions to the trailheads tell how to get there from the road listed under a county or state road heading. Road designations vary depending on the source. All road numbers in this guide are from the 1991 White River National Forest map. Road designations used on the Trails Illustrated maps are generally in agreement.

One point to keep in mind is that trails change over time. The Forest Service constructs new ones and abandons others. For this reason, always use the latest edition of any map.

Rio Blanco County Roads: 8, 10 & 17

(See Forest Road 16, Page 118)

We'll begin at the town of Meeker, west of the wilderness, in Rio Blanco County. A mile from town, heading toward Craig on State Highway 13, go east on Rio Blanco County Road 8. This paved road follows the White River through ranch country and is the primary access to the north side of the wilderness. The road between Meeker and Yampa has been designated as a Scenic Byway by the Forest Service. You come to Buford eighteen miles east of State Highway 13.

From Buford, County Road 8 follows the North Fork of the White River upstream, to the east. It's six miles past the store to County Road 12, which gives access to trails in the Marvine Creek area. Another two miles east, you reach a second road that crosses the North Fork to connect with County Road 12. Then two more miles on County Road 8 to the Lost Creek Guard Station and the end of the blacktop. Even though the road from here to the Routt County line is gravel, it's good, with a few washboard areas.

The North Fork Campground is two miles east of Lost Creek Guard Station. It is on the north, a good place to camp that's usually quiet. Another six miles takes you to Forest Road 205, the access to Trappers Lake.

County Road 8 continues east, climbing toward Ripple Creek Pass after passing Forest Road 205, another five miles to the Ripple Creek Overlook on the south. From this point, you have a broad view of the Flat Tops Wilderness. It's another mile to the 10,343-foot summit of the pass.

Rio Blanco County Roads 17 and 10

A few feet west of the Buford Store, County Road 17 goes south. This road eventually joins Interstate 70 at New Castle.

Turn left at the red buildings one mile south on County Road 17, which takes you to County Road 10. This road follows the South Fork of the White River, meandering through the broad plain of glacially deposited sediments. Deer will often be seen browsing in the hay meadows along the willow-lined stream. Elk, too. The South Fork Campground is at the end of the road, about eleven miles from Buford.

Current information on the following trails is available from:

Blanco Ranger District
White River National Forest
317 E. Market
P.O. Box 7
Meeker, Co 81649
(303) 878-4039

OYSTER LAKE TRAIL 1825

Description

This is the longest trail on the Flat Tops. It connects with several trails on the plateau, creating the possibility of many side trips if you have the time. You could also exit the wilderness by one of these trails. From the trailhead south of Buford, the route climbs quickly. Most of the 4,000-foot ascent occurs in the first five miles. Once you're on the plateau, the hike is much easier, at times, nearly level. This is a good hike to experience the extensive size of the wilderness.

Destination

Bailey Lake, Trails 1826, 2248, 2255, 2256, 1824, 1830, 1823, 1822, 1819, 1818 on the Flat Tops plateau.

Distance

Four miles to Bailey Lake, twenty-five miles to Trail 1818.

Elevation

7,000 at trailhead, 11,200 a mile west of Lost Solar Park

Directions to trailhead

0.6 miles south of Buford on County Road 17. Park at the trailhead on west side of the road. Space is limited and your vehicle is exposed.

Maps

Big Marvine Peak, Buford, Oyster Lake

The trail starts climbing as soon as you leave the county road and from there it's all uphill to Bailey Lake. In the four miles to the lake, the trail rises 1,800 feet. In the first couple of miles, you will cross private land, so stay on the trail to avoid trespassing.

The first two or three miles take you through open ground and scattered stands of scrub brush. It crosses five intermittent creeks, that is, they're usually dry except during the spring thaw. You'll have about a mile of timber to walk through before breaking into a narrow opening for the last one-half mile to Trail 1826, which takes you alongside Bailey Lake.

The Oyster Lake Trailhead, south of Buford

At the junction of 1826, Trail 1825 goes off to the east. A one-quarter mile walk takes you to Swede Lake. Both lakes have open ground that's nearly level and suitable for camping. They're supposed to contain brooks and rainbows up to twelve inches.

After leaving Swede Lake, the trail heads upward again, roughly following another intermittent drainage for a little more than a mile. Near the top of the draw, you can connect with Trail 2248,which will take you north down Papoose Creek.

From the junction with Trail 2248, 1825 turns southeast and takes you along the edge of the cliff-face above Peltier Basin. You will want to take plenty of water on this stretch to keep from getting dehydrated as none is available along the trail. If you do need to refill your canteen, White Springs is located a mile east of the trail at the head of Papoose Creek. You'll find the spring in a long, narrow meadow two miles south from the junction of Trail 2248.

As you ascend the gently sloping plateau, notice that the dropoff gradually increases from 600 feet, just above Swede Lake, to 1,200 feet where you view Peltier Lake, a mile to the west.

Hiking five miles south from Swede Lake takes you to the junction of Trail 2255, leading down Hill Creek. Clam Lake, the first available water along the trail after leaving Swede Lake, is one-half mile farther south. From Clam Lake, the trail takes an easterly direction, where you walk in the open across a grassy flat. Near the next stand of timber, Trail 2256 connects from the south.

The trail again enters the trees and descends a gentle slope. It emerges at Johnson Park, a long, narrow meadow a mile farther east on the trail. Here, you'll cross Ute Creek, which heads in Papoose Lake, one-half mile to the south.

East of Johnson Park, the trail wanders through broken country, a mix of timber and open meadows. These areas can be good places to watch for elk. You will appreciate a pleasant feature of the Flat tops on this part of the trail: it's nearly flat for sixteen miles, with only moderate changes in elevation.

From Johnson Park east, the basalt-covered plateau is pockmarked with dozens of pothole lakes, their shallow depressions scraped out by Pleistocene glaciers. The next such lake you'll come to along the trail is Oyster Lake, one-quarter mile north of the trail along Trail 1824, which gives access to West Marvine and Ute creeks to the north. If you want to camp here, try the timber on the northeast side, well away from the lake.

Past the Trail 1824 junction, the trail still continues east through the same mix of timber and meadows. As you approach Lost Solar Park, the trail begins a moderate climb, but not steep. You'll go past two small, unnamed peaks on the way to Trail 1828, which is about four miles from Oyster Lake. Near the first little molehill of a mountain, the trail reaches it zenith at 11,200 feet.

Lost Solar Park is a gently sloping, high alpine meadow. Glaciers have left the terrain rather lumpy. An abundance of moisture gives the grass a dark emerald color. July produces a plethora of wildflowers. There's a good chance of seeing elk here, either early or late in the day. At the east end of the park, a spur leads north to a group of unnamed lakes.

Past the park, the trail gets back into the timber, taking you beside several lakes tucked away in the trees and scattered about in nearby meadows. When the trail emerges from the timber, you'll come to Doe Creek Trail, three miles past the junction of Trail 1828. Going to the right here will take you down Doe Creek over a trail that is no longer maintained. A few feet farther east, Trail 1823 will lead you down Marvine Creek past the Marvine Lakes. One-quarter mile east you connect with Trail 2259, leading down to the South Fork of the White River.

Continuing east, 1825 leads through alpine tundra, past more pothole lakes and among stunted willows. Another two miles along takes you to Trail 1822 and Twin Lakes. They're named Twin Lakes because of being exactly alike except for their different shapes and one being three times as large as the other. Each lake does have an island. Looking to the east from the lakes, you will have a view of Trappers Peak, rising to a height of 12,002 feet. To the north-west is Big Marvine Peak not quite as high but still impressive at 11,879.

South of Twin Lakes, you'll se a low, broad, flat-topped hill, its slopes partially covered by timber. What you won't see from the trail are the several potholes on the top of the miniature plateau. This spot could make a good camp area as long as you keep your distance from the water.

Continuing east from Twin Lakes, the ground is nearly flat. A one-mile stretch of trail crosses only a single contour line. This high plateau is also covered with pothole lakes, though of a lesser number than the area near Oyster Lake.

From Twin Lakes, it's only two more miles to Trail 1819. At this junction, look south and you see a low, timbered slope below Trappers Peak. Hidden south of the trees is Star Lake, the largest of several shallow glacially scoured potholes. There's no trail there but you'll find it easily by heading south toward the abrupt peak, staying in the open alpine meadow until you reach the outlet stream flowing east from Star Lake.

A mile past the trail to Big Fish Lake, you come to Trail 1818. At this junction, it's three miles to Trappers Lake, all down-hill, or a mile south to Wall Lake.

Camp sites along the longest trail on the Flat Tops are available at any flat ground where you want to set your tent. Just be sure to stay at least 100 feet from the trail or water.

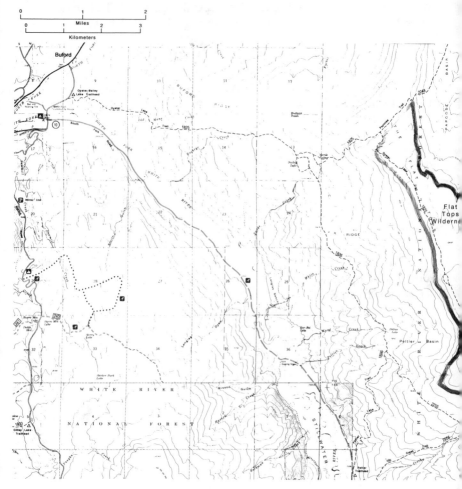

Oyster Lake Trail 1825, Part 1, and Peltier Lake Trail 1826,
East Side, Map 124: **Trails Illustrated Topo Map.**

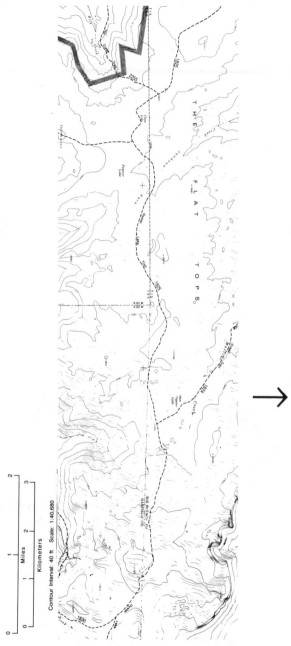

Oyster Lake Trail 1825, Part 2 . West Side,
Map 122: **Trails Illustrated Topo Map.**

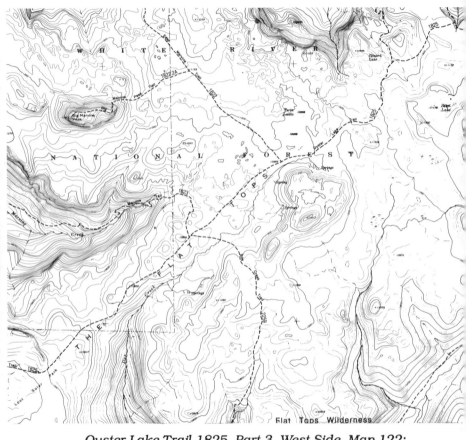

Oyster Lake Trail 1825, Part 3. West Side, Map 122:
Trails Illustrated Topo Map.

PELTIER LAKE TRAIL 1826

Description

The trail traverses a timbered slope below the plateau. It's not actually inside the Wilderness, but it is close to the boundary. There's a short, steep climb at the beginning of the hike. This trail lets you observe the variety of vegetation across the Flat Tops. Much of this hike leads through scrub oak and low willows growing on the low, west-facing slopes.

Destination

Bailey Lake, Trail 1825

Distance

3, 6.5 miles

Elevation

7,590 at trailhead, 8,892 at Trail 1825

Directions to trailhead

On County Road 10, eight miles south from County Road 17 to the trailhead on the east side of the road. Parking is available 200 yards south on the east side of the road.

Maps

Buford (See page 44)

In just a few feet, the path disappears into the trees and begins climbing as it traverses a narrow ridge and a moderately steep but short slope. To the east, you'll see a nearly vertical wall rising more than 1,000 feet to the plateau of the Flat Tops. Below you to the west, you have a view of the South Fork valley and the meandering stream as it flows south to join the North Fork. After three miles of climbing through scrub oak and low trees, you come to Peltier Lake at the west end of Peltier Basin.

The lake is shallow, but is reported to have brookies and rainbows. The north and west side of the shoreline is flat, and good for camping. The tree line on the northeast, being farther from the trail may be the best site. East of the lake and 200 feet higher, you'll find a few small ponds hidden in a clearing. One-half mile north of the lake is a meadow where you should be able to camp away from the ponds.

From Peltier Lake, the trail continues, north, traversing the west-facing slope and crossing several intermittent drainages. The last mile of the trail to Bailey Lake is across a flat, marshy in places, as it cuts through the timber. The path connects with Trail 1825 a hundred yards north of the lake.

The Oyster Lake Trail follows the rim of the plateau. The Peltier Lake Trail wanders below the vertical wall.

HILL CREEK TRAIL 2255

Description

This route takes you on a constant climb as you work your way up the scrub-covered lower slopes and timbered high country. It generally follows Hill Creek to the plateau.

Destination

Trail 1825

Distance

4 miles

Elevation

8,010 at trailhead, 10,657 at Trail 1825

Directions to trailhead

8.8 miles south on County Road 10 from County Road 17. Forest Service sign on the left reads "Hill Creek Trail Head One Mile. High Clearance Vehicles Only." The road is fine as long as it's dry. Trail 2255 heads east, uphill, from the parking area.

Maps

Buford, Oyster Lake

The trailhead is a large parking area in the open surrounded by aspen groves, and lodgepole and spruce forest. There's plenty of room here to park a pickup and horse trailer if you prefer riding rather than walking the trails. The trail begins at the east end of the parking area. One-half mile east of the trailhead, you cross Hill Creek Trail, then head up a steep slope north of the stream. Be aware that this trail is not found on USGS quads older than the 1987 photo revised edition.

After crossing the small stream, the path stays above the creek as you climb the steep slope. After three miles, the grade moderates before beginning the final climb to the plateau. From the top, it follows one of the drainages that is the head of Hill Creek. The walk through the long, narrow meadow is easy, ascending only about 200 feet between the rim and Trail 1825. The wilderness boundary is at the rim. From there, it's a mile north to the trail junction, which is a short distance northwest of Clam Lake.

Hill Creek Trail area

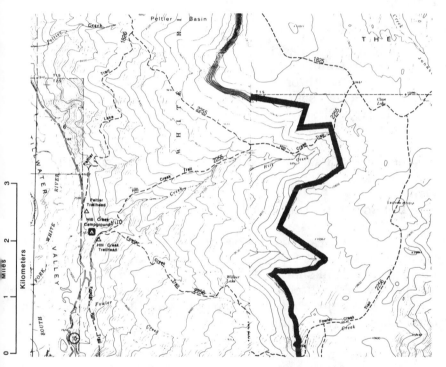

*Hill Creek Trail 2255 and Fowler Creek Trail 2256. East Side,
Map 124, West Side, Map 122:* **Trails Illustrated Topo Map.**

FOWLER CREEK TRAIL 2256

Description

    This steep trail follows Fowler Creek. It takes you into the wilderness and eventually connects with Trail 1825 near Clam Lake.

Destination

    Trail 1825

Distance

    6 miles

Elevation

    8,010 at trailhead, 11,102 at Eastview, 10,690 at Trail 1825

Directions to trailhead

    8.8 miles south on County Road 10 from County Road 17. Forest Service sign on the left reads "Hill Creek Trail Head One Mile. High Clearance Vehicles Only." The road is fine as long as it's dry. At the parking area, the road makes a loop to the west. Trail 2256 begins at the west end of the loop, where it heads uphill south, then turns east near the summit of the low ridge.

Maps

    Buford, Oyster Lake (See Page 51)

    Fowler Creek joins Hill Creek about one-half mile east of the trailhead. It's a small, fast stream flowing down a narrow draw. The Fowler Creek Trail shares the trailhead with the Hill Creek Trail. The path wanders through the timber a short distance as it climbs the nose of a broad ridge above Fowler Creek. It soon crosses an open slope as it heads uphill southeast toward Wilbur Lake, two miles from the trailhead.

    A mile farther east, the path becomes steeper as it reaches the headwall of the small draw drained by Fowler Creek. As it ascends to the plateau, you climb 600 feet in little more than one-half mile.

    Near the rim of the Wilderness plateau, the trail enters a meadow and the climb moderates as it leads through meadows broken by scattered stands of timber. A mile from the rim, the ascent flattens, following a low draw to the high point on the trail, a summit named Eastview. It overlooks a 200-foot dropoff to the east.

    From here, you continue north, where the trail enters another long, narrow meadow after a half-mile walk. The trail joins Trail 1825 after another mile to the north.

SOUTH FORK TRAIL, 1827

Description

An easy hike. The trail climbs only 1,400 feet in thirteen miles as it follows the South Fork of the White River, emerging from the deep canyon at a place named The Meadows. It can be hiked from either end. Take lightweight waders to fish the river. Several pleasant camp sites are found along the trail.

Destination

Trail 1828, Trail 1829, The Meadows

Distance

5, 7, 13 miles

Elevation

7,602 at the trailhead, 9,000 at The Meadows

Directions to trailhead

From County Road 17, go south on County Road 10 to South Fork Campground, ten miles, to the end of the road. Park at the south end of the campground.

Maps

Blair Mountain, Deep Lake, Meadow Creek Lake

The trail begins at the entrance of a deep, narrow canyon carved in massive limestone. It follows the course of the South Fork of the White River, leading you upstream and exiting the gorge at The Meadows, thirteen miles up the river.

After leaving the trailhead, you walk beside one of the most beautiful streams in the state. Following the runoff, the water is clear, flowing over a bed of black and red basalt, and white limestone boulders. The stream is broad, having numerous deep holes, hiding places for trout. If you approach the water carefully, you'll also see rainbow and cutthroat that occasionally rise to inhale a tasty-looking insect from the surface. A few feet from the parking area is a wooden bridge crossing the river. The path on the other side leads to Cliff Lake and Spring Cave, a hole in the limestone extending several miles. It's about a mile up the trail and worth the detour.

About three miles from the campground the river narrows, being squeezed by the canyon walls, as it plunges over a short series of cascades. Be sure to take your camera for this scenic spot.

Above the cascades, the canyon opens a bit and the stream channel broadens. Another two miles of easy walking takes you to Lost Solar Creek and Trail 1828. The land and cabins here are private, the ownership dating back years prior to creation of the Wilderness. The area is marked. Through this section, you must stay on the trail to avoid trespassing.

South Fork of the White River near the South Fork Trailhead.

A mile upstream from Lost Solar Park, the trail wanders through timber at the bottom of the deep gorge. Another mile takes you to Park Creek and Trail 1829, which follows the creek up to the plateau.

Above Park Creek, the canyon walls become steeper, nearly vertical in appearance. Here, the trail wanders a short distance from the river, far enough that you'll miss an especially scenic narrow section. This one is about eight miles from the trailhead. Here, the stream has cut a trough through the resistant granite, creating an angler's frustration. The long narrow pool is deep; too deep to wade. Steep granite walls make the water unreachable from either side. A pool created by a log jam at the upper end and a deep plunge at the outlet make either approach difficult. The pool is photogenic, though.

In this narrow portion of the canyon, the river meanders through shallow riffles, and plunges over boulders. Deep pools form at bends, creating trout holding water. A little farther upstream, the gradient increases and willows growing along either bank make it difficult to approach the water; very frustrating if you're an angler. A little farther upstream is a small falls, not very high but large enough to be noted on topo maps. Above the falls, the gradient flattens and the trail climbs less steeply. Near the falls is a wooden gate across the trail. Be sure to close it after passing.

The final three miles of the trail is an easy walk past lush meadows and vertical limestone walls. The climb is only 120 feet in that distance. Aspen groves shade the bench above the river. You pass through several more gates along the way. Across from the White River Resort, near the end of your hike, is a fenced pasture in which the resort sometimes keeps horses. Be sure to close the gates so the horses don't wander.

Also across from the resort, the trail weaves through a patch of willows that grow along an unnamed trickle coming off the plateau from the north. The tiny stream has sufficient flow to flood the trail here, but by clinging to the edge of the path and the brush, you can keep your feet dry. You will see a path leading up the side of the canyon on the west side of these willows, too. This is Budge's Trail and takes you up a steep climb onto the plateau.

From here, it's less than one-half mile to the east end of the trail. A wooden foot bridge takes you across the river to a parking lot a mile west of The Meadows Trailhead.

Camping along the river is a pleasant experience and there are sites along the trail. Pick your site with care, though. High ground is suggested as heavy rains upstream can raise the water level quickly. Also, remember the 100-foot distance from water to your camp. The only exception to open camping is the area at Lost Solar Creek, which is private land.

LOST SOLAR TRAIL 1828

Description

The canyon the trail follows shows the contrasting geology of the Flat Tops. It was formed by faulting and erosion rather than by glaciers. It's a long, but not too steep climb except in a few places.

Destination

Lost Solar Park, Trail 1825

Distance

8 miles

Elevation

7,904 at Trail 1827, 10,750 at Trail 1825

Directions to trail

From South Fork CG, take Trail 1827 along the South Fork of the White River upstream five miles to trail. You can also reach this trail from The Meadows, and Trail 1830 on the plateau.

Maps

Big Marvine Peak, Blair Mountain, Oyster Lake

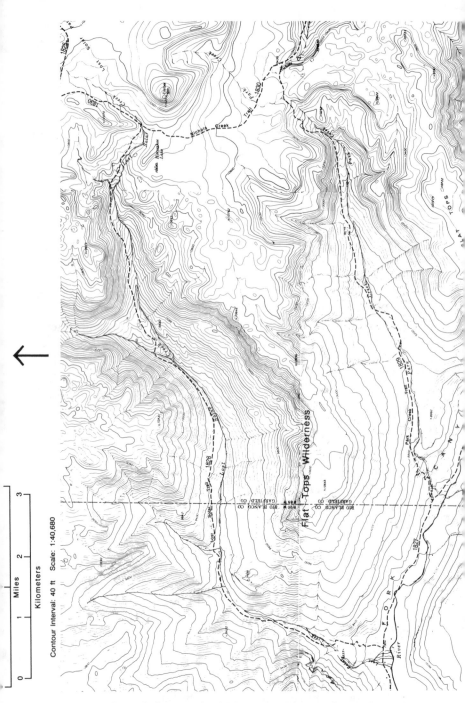

Lost Solar Trail 1828 and Park Creek Trail 1829.
Map 122 West: **Trails Illustrated Topo Map.**

Near the junction of the South Fork and Lost Solar Trails.

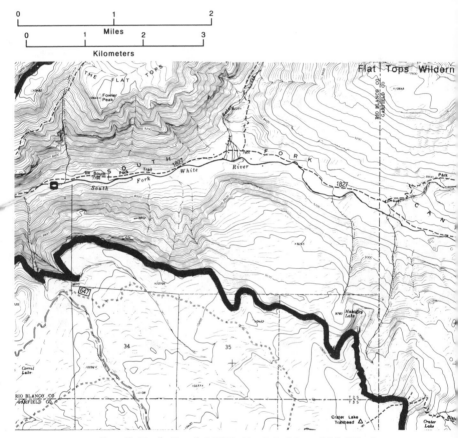

South Fork Trail 1827, Part 1, Map 122 West
Trails Illustrated Topo Map.

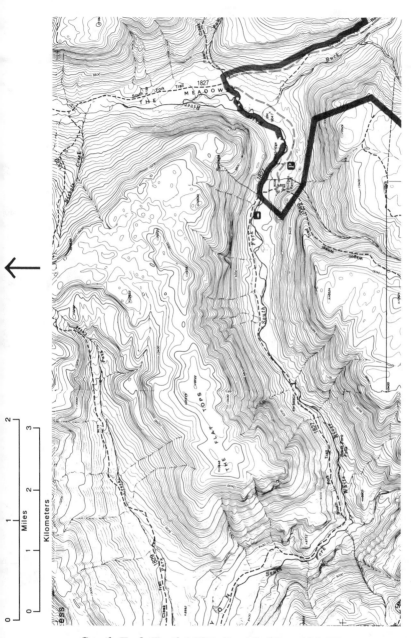

South Fork Trail 1827, Part 2. Map 122 West
Trails Illustrated Topo Map.

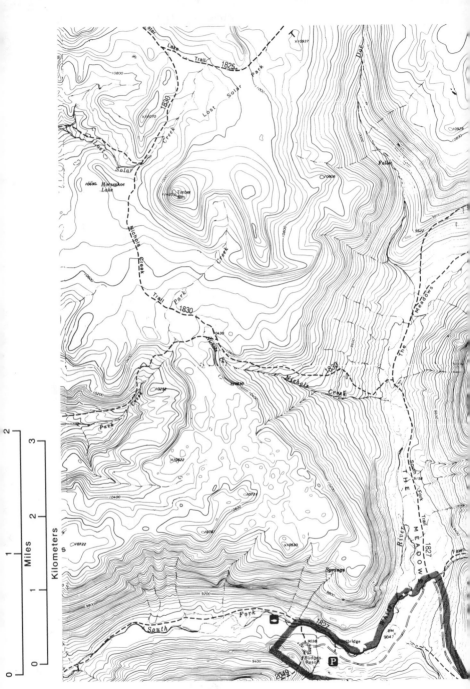

South Fork Trail 1827, Part 3, Map 122 West
Trails Illustrated Topo Map.

The steep-sided walls are a prominent feature found in the South Fork of the White River canyon. From the bottom, access to the plateau appears off-limits to hikers. Fortunately, incisions have been made in the rugged landscape, the result of fracturing and erosion of the rock. During the construction of the Flat Tops, the rock was broken by faulting. Natural processes of weathering enlarged these fractures, creating V-shaped canyons, in contrast to the U-shaped valley of the South Fork, formed by moving layers of ice. Lost Solar Creek is one of the drainages formed by faulting of the rock. The resultant valley offers the hiker relatively easy access to the top.

The trail begins at the confluence of Lost Solar Creek and the South Fork, among a group of cabins. The land here is private so stay on the trail. It follows the creek along the bottom of the deep V-shaped canyon. Because of the steep sides, there are few suitable campsites until you are five miles up the trail from the South Fork. Here at the confluence of Lost Solar and a small, unnamed creek that heads in the small canyon to the north, the ground is flat enough for camping.

The grade is gentle most of the way as the path traverses the left side of the canyon. Past the confluence of Lost Solar and the unnamed stream, the trail climbs again, a bit more steeply this time. It finally emerges from the canyon in sight of Timber Mountain and Lost Solar Park. Here you connect with Trail 1828.

Camp sites are limited along this trail. but once you are on the flat, you will find meadows where you will want to set up your tent. The unnamed creek, which joins Lost Solar Creek from the north, has spots large enough for a backpack tent.

PARK CREEK TRAIL 1829

Description
Similar to Lost Solar Trail 1828 but a bit shorter.
Destination
Park Creek, Trail 1830
Distance
5 miles
Elevation
8,131 at the South Fork, 10,430 at Trail 1830
Directions to trail
Seven miles from South Fork Campground up Trail 1827, or six miles downstream from Budge's Resort on Trail 1827, accessed from Forest Road 600.

Big Marvine Peak, Blair Mountain, Deep Lake (See Page 56)

The Park Creek Trail leaves the South Fork Trail here.

Park Creek descends another canyon carved by glaciers. The trail departs the South Fork in a broad area of the valley and climbs rather abruptly for the first one-half miles before leveling out. For the next three miles, the ascent is gradual as the path meanders through the trees and open meadows while crossing the creek several times. As you approach the head of the canyon, the way steepens. Near the upper end of the canyon you'll find a falls. It's not large but is scenic. The last mile ascends quickly, requiring switchbacks to get up the steep head wall before you emerge on the flat. A short walk through the open meadow takes you to Trail 1830. If you want to camp along the trail, you'll find places in the wooded flat middle section of the canyon.

PAPOOSE CREEK TRAIL 2248

Description

The trail follows Papoose Creek the first two miles, leading through dense timber and narrow meadows along the creek. The hike takes you through Papoose Basin before ascending

Late-summer elderberries along the Papoose Trail.

the steep wall to the west, giving access to the wilderness once
on the plateau.

Destination

Trail 1825

Distance

6 miles.

Elevation

7,630 at trailhead, 9,920 at Trail 1825

Directions to trailhead

Six miles east of the Buford Store, go right on County Road 12,
then one mile east to County Road 119. Turn right, south,
about one mile to a junction. Continue straight ahead, south,
to the trailhead parking area on the left, 0.7 miles from County
Road 12. The trailhead is located one-quarter mile past the
parking area, left of the entrance to Pollard's Ute Lodge. **The
White River National Forest map erroneously shows County
Road 119 as County Road 75, however trailhead location
is correctly marked.**

Maps

Buford, Fawn Creek, Lost Park

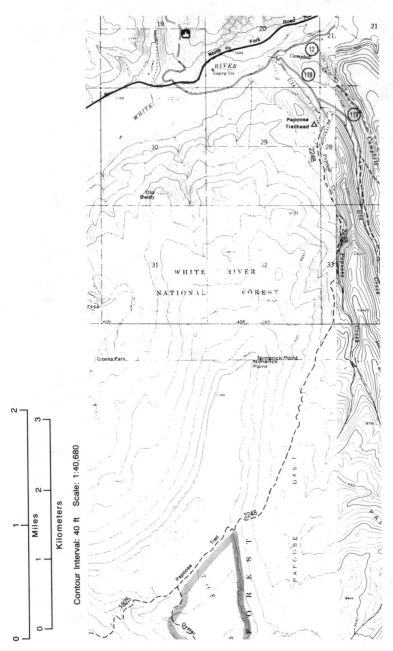

Papoose Creek Trail 2248. East Side, Map 124,
West Side, Map 122: **Trails Illustrated Topo Map.**

This trail begins by following Papoose Creek up its small, timbered draw from the first mile. Then the main trail leaves the water while a spur continues up the creek.

After climbing to 8,800 feet, the trail enters Papoose Basin, a small park with scattered stands of timber and sloping meadows. Looking to the west, you'll see a steep wall, rising some 700 feet. The trail leads up that wall. Once on top, though, the walk is just a stroll through the meadow across a narrow plateau, where you connect with Trail 1825 and enter the wilderness.

Carry plenty of water. There's none available between Papoose Creek and Swede Lake, a distance of about five miles.

UTE CREEK TRAIL 1824

Description

This route parallels Ute Creek to the wilderness boundary five miles from the trailhead. Much of the trail is up a moderate grade until reaching the steep wall leading to the plateau. Here, the ascent is steep but short. The trail soon crosses West Marvine Creek and follows it to Oyster Lake and Trail 1825.

Destination

Trail 1825

Distance

9 miles

Elevation

7,760 at trailhead, 10,701 at junction with Trail 1825.

Directions to trailhead

Six miles east of the Buford Store, go right on County Road 12, then one mile east to County Road 119. Turn right, south, one-half mile to a junction. Go left on an undesignated Forest Road to a group of privately-owned summer cabins. Park on the right beside Ute Creek, then walk south on the road to the trailhead beside the bridge.

Maps

Lost Park, Oyster Lake

Oyster Lake, near the Oyster Lake and Ute Creek trails.

Ute Creek Trail 1824, East Side 124, West Side. 122:
Trails Illustrated Topo Map.

This trail takes you on one of the higher climbs of any in the Flat Tops: nearly 3,000 feet. Immediately after leaving the parking area, you'll enter the first of many long but narrow meadows as you begin your ascent.

The first half of the trail closely follows Ute Creek. The stream is small, its banks lined with brush. It does have brookies and cutthroats, though.

You enter the Wilderness five miles from the trailhead. So far, the climb has been steady but not steep. For the next 1 1/2 miles, the climb gets more serious, rising 1,200 feet, 600 of which occurs in the last half-mile. Once you're on top, though, the walk is easy.

South and west of the trail are more than a dozen pothole lakes. The ground is mostly flat, making for good camp sites near the trees.

You'll come to the West Marvine Trail, which leads down West Marvine Creek to Marvine Campground, seven miles from the trailhead. Most of this north-bound trail is no longer maintained.

Continuing on south, the trail stays in the open the last two miles, leading past Oyster Lake and to Trail 1825.

MARVINE LAKES TRAIL 1823

Description

This is another trail that gets you onto the plateau. It's not a difficult hike, as the trail has only a few moderately steep sections as it ascends the scenic, glacially carved valley. Be sure to take your fishing rod as there are numerous places to fish along the way. Because of the several lodges near lower Marvine Creek, this is a popular trail for horse pack trips. On top, you can take your choice of several trails for a different return route.

Destination

Slide Lake, Marvine Lakes, Trail 1825

Distance

3, 6, 11.5, miles

Elevation

8,160 at trailhead, 10,954 at junction with Trail 1825

Directions to trailhead

Eight miles east of the Buford Store, go right (south) across the bridge to County Road 12. Go left past Fritzlan's Cafe. The road turns south near Adams Lodge and follows Marvine Creek. The trailhead is 5.5 miles past Fritzlan's and one-half mile past the East Marvine CG. The trail heads right of the horse corral.

Maps

Big Marvine Peak, Deep Lake, Lost Park, Oyster Lake

Lower Marvine Lake on the Marvine Trail

As you begin your hike along this trail, you head south from the trailhead and horse loading area on the east side of the road in sight of the campground. The path crosses a couple of small ridges, which fortunately are not too high or steep, giving you a chance to adjust to the load on your back. After about a mile, the trail descends slightly to follow Marvine Creek.

The gradual climb along Marvine Creek is not difficult. Much of the way, you'll walk in the open, below a timbered slope above you to the east, and below nearly vertical walls. Marvine Creek will be in view to the west most of the way. It's a small stream that is home to small brookies, cutthroat, and rainbow trout. A few ponds create deep holes for the fish. The water is clear, though, and a careful approach is needed to avoid spooking them when the surface is smooth.

Three miles up the trail you come to Slide Lake, looking much like a giant beaver pond, which it isn't. The lake is full of brookies up to eight or nine inches, all eager to hit a fly. The clarity of the water is deceitful. You won't be able to wade out very far, even with hip boots.

To the east above the lake, you'll be able to see the steep buttresses forming the foundation for Rat Mountain, its summit reaching above 11,000 feet. Early in the summer, you'll see water falls plunging off the plateau, dropping several hundred feet.

The trail is slightly challenging as it crosses the outlet of Slide Lake. Difficulty of the crossing depends on the season. During runoff, it may be good to carry lightweight waders so you can stay dry while wading the thigh-deep water that runs over the trail. You can rock hop along the outlet side of Slide Lake, but this can be tricky when the water is still high. On the downstream side of the trail, from time to time, someone places a log across the stream for a bridge. Don't count on finding one, though, as spring runoff periodically removes it. After runoff, crossing on the rocks at the outlet is easy and you can keep dry without waders, provided you don't slip.

From Slide Lake, the trail begins climbing faster but still isn't steep. A mile from the stream crossing below Slide Lake, you come to another, a creek coming off the high ground to the right. This one is much easier. Below the point where the stream flows across the trail is a single log that can be used to cross. The small stream, however, is shallow enough to wade if you have waterproof boots, even early in the season. Later in the year, it may be dry as the stream doesn't run continuously except in very wet years.

The next mile of trail climbs a bit faster, but still isn't difficult unless your pack is heavy. You'll pass three small barren ponds on the right before entering the timber again. A half-mile farther, the trail rejoins Marvine Creek, which it left above Slide Lake. One-half mile below Lower Marvine Lake, there's a wooden gate across the trail, which is no problem for hikers to walk around. At the stream, you'll see a horse trail on the other bank. It connects with the main trail one-quarter mile upstream. Hikers, however, can stay on the west bank of the stream, following it through a narrow draw having steep sides along the water. The passage is difficult early in the season before the snow has melted. Use the horse trail then.

A short distance upstream, the trail breaks into the open beside a quarter-mile long beaver pond. A couple of hundred yards above the pond is a crude log bridge that allows you to cross the stream without getting wet. Now, you're almost within sight of Lower Marvine Lake, one of two glacially formed impoundments. For high lakes, they're large; the lower is 65 acres, the upper, 88. Fishing in them is good for small brookies and cutthroats. Level campsites are limited.

North of Lower Marvine and east of the trail are two lakes hidden in the pine and spruce forest. The path is well defined where it leaves the main trail, 1823, just north of the beaver pond. Pine Isle and Ruby Lakes both have fish. There are several good camp sites along the shoreline of Pine Isle.

Trail 1823 follows the north shoreline of Lower Marvine Lake.

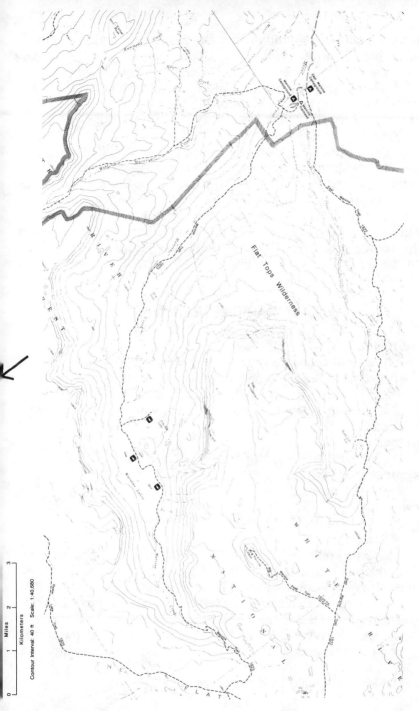

Marvine Trail 1823, East Marvine Trail 1822 & Big Marvine Peak 1822.2A, Map 122 West — **Trails Illustrated Topo Map.**

The upper lake is separated from the lower by a string of small, shallow ponds. At the west end of Upper Marvine Lake is a small island, having an old beaver lodge. Along this end of the lake, the glacier piled basalt boulders around the shore when the dam was formed of the rubble. Lichens growing on the rock indicate many years of exposure. It takes about fifty years for the lichens to get established.

One of the area resorts has a camp established at the upper lake. When you enter the trees along the north shore, you'll find a wooden gate across the trail. Keep it closed so the lodge's horses don't wander.

Continuing on up the trail past Upper Marvine, the walls of the glacially carved gorge begin to close in on you. The climb gets a little steeper, too. Switchbacks make it less strenuous. You come onto the flat after 3 more miles of hiking, one-half mile north of Trail 1825.

EAST MARVINE TRAIL 1822

Description

A long trail that gives access to the Little Marvine Peaks and Big Marvine Peak and several lakes. The path crosses a large, glacially scoured valley. The wall of ice left the terrain rough and uneven below the nearly vertical walls on the east and south.

Destination

Mary Loch Lake, Big Marvine Peak Trail, Trail 1825

Distance

7, 9, 10.5 miles

Elevation

8,081 at trailhead, 11,155 at Big Marvine Peak Trail, 10,989 at Trail 1825

Directions to trailhead

Eight miles east of the Buford Store, go right (south) across the bridge to County Road 12. Go left past Fritzlan's Cafe. The road turns south near Adams Lodge and follows Marvine Creek. The trailhead is 5.5 miles past Fritzlan's and one-half mile past the East Marvine CG. The trail heads left of the horse corral. You can also access the trail from East Marvine Campground.

Maps

Big Marvine Peak, Lost Park (See Page 71)

The Little Marvine Peaks from the East Marvine Trail.

From the trailhead beside the horse corral, you walk down the often muddy path to cross the stream. It's big enough that getting to the other side would be a challenge without the bridge. For the first mile, the trail follows the path of East Marvine Creek, a boisterous, fast moving creek having few quiet pools. In that first mile, you climb 500 feet. You also enter a long, narrow valley, having open slopes. Straight ahead, to the south, you have your first view of the three Little Marvine Peaks. Leaving the creek, you follow another draw up through the timber past Johnson Lake, which is rumored to have a few lunkers hiding in its shallow waters. By that point, you've gone two more miles and ascended another 400 feet.

The lake sits in a small opening in the forest. The water is clear, the bottom green from the moss. Past the lake, you'll continue your upward path, wandering through dense forest and small scattered parks. One-quarter mile from Johnson Lake, you come to Trail 1820.1B, leading south to Big Ridge. The junction is 25 yards past a spring that emerges beside the trail. It enters dense forest after crossing a small park one-half mile past the junction. At the edge of the trees, you cross a small creek that will be challenging early in the year.

A mile farther, you hike into a wet area having several small lakes nearby. Guthrie, Rainbow, and Shallow Lakes are the only ones named. All are reported to have fish. The ground northeast of the trail is hummocky and uneven, left this way at the end of the last ice age. When the glaciers receded, they also left the area pockmarked with many small ponds and lakes. This rough ledge is covered with stands of timber broken by extensive meadows.

A mile up from Shallow Lake is Mary Loch Lake, hidden from the trail by a small ridge. It is surrounded by timber. The wooded flat on the east side offers level camp sites. Shortly before reaching the spur trail leading to the lake, the main trail again meets Marvine Creek. Here it runs through a long, narrow flat. Its flow is less rambunctious then below.

Past the Mary Loch Lake spur, you now begin serious climbing. From the 9,800-foot park northeast of the lake, you climb to 11,000 feet in little more than a mile. Once you climb out, though, the walk is over one of the flattest areas of the Flat Tops. You'll see why the place received its name. The ground is nearly devoid of contours here. Take a look back to the north, where you have a panoramic view of the plateau and the Little Marvine Peaks. Four miles to the east, you'll see Trappers Peak with Big Marvine rising abruptly in front of you to the southwest.

A mile past the top of the canyon, you come to a side trail leading to the summit of Big Marvine Peak. This 2-mile detour takes you to one of the higher points on the Flat Tops at 11,879 feet. 1.5 miles past the detour, you arrive at the junction of Trail 1825, a few yards from Twin Lakes.

BIG MARVINE PEAK TRAIL 1822.2A

Description

This trail takes you to the top of Big Marvine Peak, a prominent feature of the Flat Tops Wilderness. The peak is visible
from many vantage points. The mountain was one of several
volcanic vents which extruded lava only a few million years
ago, or perhaps a bit more recently. It's one bit of evidence of
the relatively young age of the Flat Tops Plateau. The east half
of the peak appears rather solid, in contrast with the western
flank, which is covered with rubble from slides. Big Marvine is
a typical mountain of this Wilderness, being massive but rising less than 1,000 feet above the plateau. It's not the height,
though, that's impressive as much as the massiveness of the
block of basalt that forms the peak. After crossing the plateau
from the main trail, the route up the peak ascends the steep
east slope, the climb made somewhat easier by the switchbacks.
On top, you will be able to appreciate the vastness of the Wilderness as you scan the plateau.

Destination

Big Marvine Peak summit

Distance

2 miles

Elevation

11,155 at trail junction, 11,879 on Big Marvine Peak

Directions to trailhead

Eight miles from East Marvine Creek Trailhead, two miles from
Trail 1825.

Maps

Big Marvine Peak (See Page 71)

Big Marvine Peak

BIG RIDGE TRAIL 1820

Description

    The trail follows a feature known as Big Ridge. The first three miles is a steady climb. Once on the ridge, parks are interspersed among the timber. Only the last mile of the trail lies within the Wilderness. This trail is popular for horse trips from the nearby lodges.

Destination

    Trail 1820.1B, Sable Lake, Trail 1821

Distance

    5,7, 9 miles.

Elevation

    7,550 at trailhead, 10,161 east of Sable Lake

Directions to trailhead

    Eight miles east of the Buford Store, go right (south) across bridge to County Road 12, then east one mile, past Adams Lodge. The trailhead is next to a sign for Lost Creek Outfitters. Parking is limited.

Maps

    Lost Park, Ripple Creek

Big Ridge Trailhead

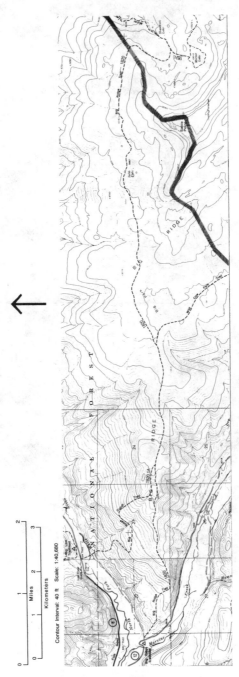

Big Ridge Trail 1820 & Big Ridge Cut-off Trail 1820.
1A, Map 122 West — **Trails Illustrated Topo Map.**

The trail starts climbing at the parking lot, following the nose of Big Ridge for nearly five miles to Big Park. In this distance, you walk through heavy timber and scattered open meadows. The climb flattens across Big Park, where you come to the junction of Wild Cow Park Trail 1820.1B

The next two miles wander through Big Park, a broad meadow having a scattering of timber. the Big Ridge Trail then begins a second ascent that takes you to Sable Lake, seven miles from your starting point.

Pack plenty of water as there is no source between the trailhead and the lake, other than Red Spring, which is not on the map. The wooded land is nearly flat, north and east of the lake, making it a good choice for a campsite. Sable is a small lake having an east-west orientation. It sits on a shelf below Sable Point, a near-vertical wall one mile to the south. Sable Point is prominent landmark, seen from other areas of the north side of the Wilderness. The lake has large cutthroats that can be picky about what they eat and when they eat it.

Going east from Sable Lake, the trail climbs less than 200 feet before beginning a gradual descent to trail 1821, two miles farther. It joins the Mirror Lake Trail one-half mile east of Mirror Lake in an opening along the nose of a small ridge.

If your destination is Sable Lake, the hike will be shorter by coming in on Trail 1821, the Mirror Lake Trail. The junction is marked with a sign reading Big Ridge Trail

Some older maps show Trail 1820 descending a steep slope using switchbacks to connect with Trail 1821. This portion is no longer maintained as downed timber on the trail has not been cleared for several years. You can still hike it but the going will be rough.

WILD COW PARK TRAIL 1820.1B

Description

A short connecting trail that has little change in elevation. There's no water along this route.

Destination

Connects Trails 1820 and 1822

Distance

4 miles

Elevation

9,570 at Trail 1820, 9,480 at Trail 1822

Directions to trail

Five miles east on Trail 1820, or three miles east on Trail 1822.

Maps

Lost Park, Trails Illustrated Map 122 - Flat Tops NE Trappers Lake

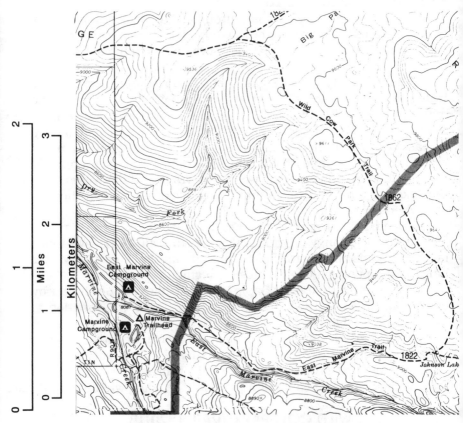

Wild Cow Park Trail 1820.1B. Map 122
*West —***Trails Illustrated Topo Map.**

Maps

Lost Park, Trails Illustrated Map 122 - Flat Tops NE Trappers Lake

This trail heads south five miles east of the Big Ridge Trailhead. It crosses the west end of Big Park, a large meadow. The first two miles take you through open parks and the edges of stands of timber. Elevation changes are moderate, making the stroll pleasant. At two miles, you enter the Wilderness. From here to Trail 1822, the ground is hummocky, the result of having glaciers do the landscaping. You connect with the trail a short distance east of Johnson Lake, the first source of water since leaving the Big Ridge Trailhead.

This trail does not appear on the USGS Lost Park quad. It's listed on the 1991 White River National Forest map as Trail 1820. 1B and on the Trails Illustrated map as Trail 1862, the correct USFS designation.

BIG RIDGE CUTOFF TRAIL 1820. 1A

Description

An alternate route to Trail 1820 and Big Ridge. The trailhead is on private land and not accessible without permission. The forest boundary is about 0.1 mile south of the river. From this point, the trail ascends the steep north slope of Big Ridge, climbing 600 feet before levelling out some. The trail swings eastward, still climbing but not so severely. After crossing the slope, it turns south again and ascends to Big Ridge.

Destination

Trail 1820

Distance

2 miles

Elevation

7,599 at County Road 8, 9,030 at Trail 1820

Directions to trailhead

Twelve miles east of the Buford Store on County Road 8, then, 0.1 mile past the Lost Creek Guard Station. The trail is south of County Road 8.

Maps

Trails Illustrated Map 122 - Flat Tops NE Trappers Lake. This trail is not shown on the USGS Lost Park quad. (See Page 80)

Forest Road 205

Forest Road 205 goes south, ending at Trappers Lake, seventeen miles east of Buford. The road gives access to Forest Road 206, Picket Pin Trail Head, Himes Peak Campground, Skinny Fish Trail Head, Trappers Lake Lodge, Trappers Outlet Trail Head, Trappers Lake campgrounds, and Wall Lake and Scotts Bay trailheads.

MIRROR LAKE TRAIL 1821

Description

The trail has several steep sections, made easier by switchbacks. Mirror Lake is close enough to do the round trip in a day without rushing. This is a popular route for trail rides.

Destination

Trail 1820, Shamrock Lake, Mirror Lake, Sable Lake

Distance

2.5, 3, 5 miles

Elevation

8,380 at trailhead, 10,040 at Mirror Lake

Directions to trailhead

South on Forest Road 205 0.3 miles to Forest Road 206. The trailhead and parking area is about one-quarter mile to the west.

Maps

Ripple Creek

Mirror Lake at the end of the Mirror Lake Trail.

The trail begins a quarter-mile from Forest Road 205. It leads the hiker down a gentle incline through an open meadow on the way to the North Fork of the White River. After one-quarter mile, the path goes through a gate onto private land owned by the Rio Blanco Ranch. Stay on the trail as numerous signs warn of severe consequences for straying. Also, watch for cattle that graze in the meadow. Remember to respect private property.

After crossing a wooden bridge, the trail begins to climb. A short distance beyond, you enter the coniferous forest and the Wilderness. Make certain to close the gate.

While the trail to Mirror Lake is a constant climb, the grade is not difficult. The few steep sections use switchbacks to make the walk easier. Most of the narrow path is shaded by the trees, making the stroll pleasant, especially on warm, dry days.

After a 2.5-mile hike, you will enter a small clearing. To the left, below the path, lies Shamrock Lake, so named because of the translucent green color of the water. Pause a few moments to watch the numerous eight and ten-inch brookies enjoy a meal of insects they find on the lake's surface, some exuberantly jumping out of the water as they feed. The angling hiker or rider may be tempted to rig up a fly rod. Try a small, dark-colored pattern.

After passing Shamrock, you come to the junction of Trail 1820. A sign reading Big Ridge Trail marks the junction. Now, you have only two more small rises to cross before reaching your destination. Your first view of Mirror Lake comes as you cross the last low rise. Ideally, the sky will be clear, the wind calm, showing a perfect reflection of the nearly vertical 1,400-foot wall standing along the lake's southwest margin. This is the time to pause, remove your pack and dig out a camera. Then sit awhile and enjoy the scene.

Again, the angler will be induced to make an effort to catch a few of the many small brookies seen swimming along the shoreline. They're susceptible to both lures and flies. A few appear emaciated but most are fat and sassy and eager to take a Rio Grande King or other fly of your choice.

The majority of Mirror Lake's shoreline is open and it's easy to circumnavigate the crude path around it. Most people do this as a day hike, but you will find a level meadow to camp, east of the lake and south of the trail.

On the east side of Mirror Lake, a trail heads east toward Paradise Creek. It descends gradually for the first 1.5 miles, then follows sharp switchbacks to descend to the creek. It follows the stream down to the confluence with the North Fork of the White River. Be aware, though, that if you take this route, you will trespass on the Rio Blanco Ranch when you leave the wilderness. This area

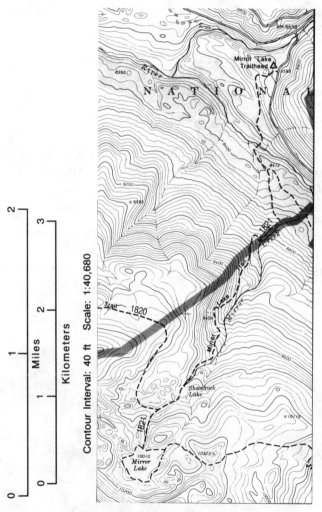

Mirror Lake Trail 1821. Map 122, West
— Trails Illustrated Topo Map.

of the ranch is not open for public use so you may want to avoid using the Paradise Creek trail.

BIG FISH TRAIL 1819

Description

This is an especially scenic trail. It follows Big Fish Creek up a broad U-shaped valley. Don't forget your camera on this hike. If you enjoy horses, this is a good trail to ride.

Destination

Trail 2262, Big Fish Lake, Trail 1877, Trail 1825

Distance

2, 4, 5, 7 miles

Elevation

8,780 at trailhead, 10,930 at junction of Trail 1825

Directions to trailhead

Seventeen miles east of Buford, go south on Forest Road 205 4.4 miles to Himes Peak Campground. Park at the north end of the campground by the horse unloading area.

Maps

Big Marvine Peak, Ripple Creek (See page 89)

The Big Fish Trail follows this valley.

You'll park at the Himes Peak CG in the shadow of Himes Peak, two miles to the south. This prominent landmark reaches a height of 11,201 feet. As you hike the trail, you will rarely stray from sight of this peak.

Leaving the campground, you follow a meandering trail down to the North Fork of the White River, which is here little more than a creek in size. On the other side of the stream, the trail begins a gradual climb, paralleling Big Fish Creek. The junction of Trail 2262, which leads to Boulder Lake, is two miles from the trailhead. While you walk through the meadow above the junction, look to the left, to the slope north of Himes Peak to catch a view of Bessies Falls.

In the first four miles of your hike, you stroll through a mix of timber, open meadows, and willows on the way to Big Fish Lake. The lake is stocked with rainbows averaging ten inches in length. Campsite choices leave much to be desired. There are small flat spots on the east but they're close to the trail. The ground at the north and south ends of the lake is level but in the open. The timber on the west side could be your best choice.

A mile above Big Fish, a crude trail leads to Gwendolyn Lake, hidden among the trees on a small ledge a mile south of Big Fish Lake. The lake is reported to have cutthroats.

After passing the junction, the trail wanders along the edge of a large meadow before entering the timber and beginning a serious climb. A mile or so past Big Fish Lake, you encounter a single long switchback.

Along the switchback, you connect with Trail 1877, which heads off to the northeast, uphill through the trees. This path leads to Florence Lake and around the north side of Himes peak. You'll find camp sites along the lake. It's said the lake is fishless. The detour is still worthwhile, though, as this is among the more scenic areas on the Flat Tops — if that is really possible.

Another mile along the trail, past Trail 1877, takes you to a steep, heartpounding climb. You'll go from 10,200 to 10,760 within one-half mile. And while it may be repetitious, it's just another one-half mile up a slight rise to the flat and Trail 1825.

BOULDER LAKE TRAIL 2262

Description
   This trail takes you up a pretty good climb but the emerald green lake at the end makes it worth the effort.
Destination
   Boulder Lake
Distance
   3 miles

Elevation

8,930 at Trail 1819, 9,770 at Boulder Lake

Directions to trail

Two miles up Trail 1819 from Himes Peak Campground.

Maps

Ripple Creek (See Page 89)

The trail takes off to the west from Trail 1819 at the edge of a sloping meadow. You descend a short distance to cross Big Fish Creek, then begin climbing. The hill is steep but switchbacks moderate the grade as you ascend.

After a two-mile walk, you come out of the timber onto a large flat opening. Through the middle of the clearing is the small stream flowing out of Boulder Lake. You first see the lake from above. The clear water appears green from the mossy bottom. It is home to rainbows that can reach twelve inches in length. The ground is flat enough on the north and south sides for camping. Watch for elk in this area.

Less than a mile to the south is Doris Lake. No trail leads to it but by following the meadow east of Boulder Lake up the moderately-steep slope, and following the contour around the nose of the timbered ridge, you should find it. The best campsite is probably the meadow south of the lake. Be sure to stay well back from the water. The Forest Service has tentative plans for a trail connecting Boulder and Mirror Lakes.

LAKE OF THE WOODS TRAIL 2263

Description

This new trail creates additional hiking opportunities near the Trappers Lake Campground. It's an easy walk to help you get adjusted to the altitude. Lake of the Woods is a very pretty lake, surrounded by tall spruce and pines, having small brookies.

Destination

Trail 2261, Lake of the Woods

Distance

1/2, 1 mile.

Elevation

9,250 at Forest Road 205, 9,010 at Lake of the Woods

Directions to trailhead

Seventeen miles east of Buford, go south 6.7 miles on Forest Road 205 to Skinny Fish Trailhead. Park here and walk back along the road past Skinny Fish Creek to trailhead.

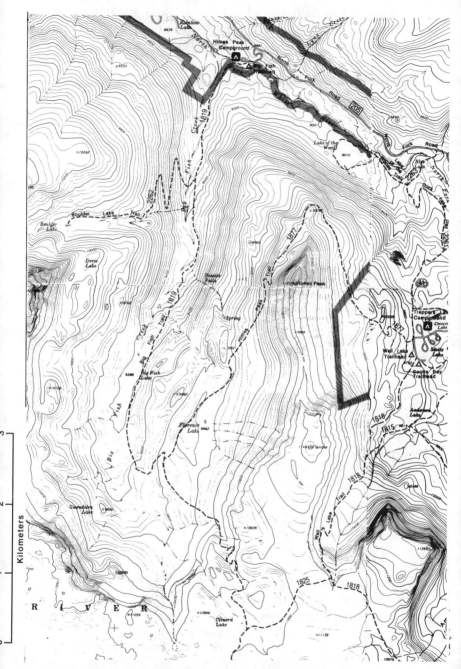

Big Fish Trail 1819, Boulder Lake Trail 2262 and Himes Peak Trail 1877, Map 122, West & 122, East
— **Trails Illustrated Topo Map.**

A second route to the lake is not marked. Park along the road, six miles from CR 8 and walk west to the lake. You'll often see other cars parked here.

Maps

Trappers Lake (See page 91)

DUCK LAKE TRAIL 2261

Description

This is one of several trails accessed from Trappers Lake Campground. It connects a bike path out of the campground with Trail 2263. A short and very easy walk.

Destination

Lake of the Woods Trail

Distance

1 mile.

Elevation

9,520 at bike path, 9,240 at Trail 2263

Directions to trailhead

Seventeen miles east of Buford, go south 7.8 miles on Forest road 205 to Forest Road 209 and Trappers Lake Campground.

Maps

Trails Illustrated Flat Tops NE Trappers Lake Map 122 (See Page 91)

HIMES PEAK TRAIL 1877

Description

This trail takes you around the north side of Himes Peak and along Florence Lake. It was constructed in 1993.

Destination

Florence Lake, Trail 1819

Distance

4, 5 miles.

Elevation

9,755 at Wall Lake Trailhead, 10,400 west of Himes Peak.

Directions to trailhead

Seventeen miles east of Buford, go south 7.8 miles on forest Road 205 to Trappers Lake Lodge. Forest Road 209 goes right across the North fork of the White River, across from the lodge. It's 1.7 miles from the turnoff to the Wall Lake Trailhead. Park here and walk back on the road to the turn to pick up the trail, which heads west.

Maps

Trappers Lake (See page 89)

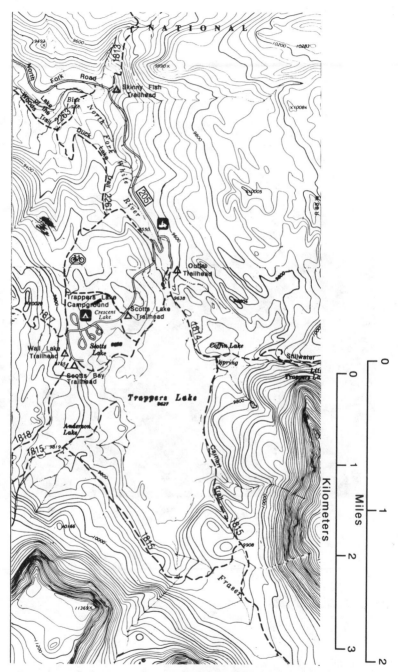

Lake of the Woods Trail 2263, Duck Lake Trail 2261 and Carhart Trail 1815. Map 122 East — **Trails Illustrated Topo Map.**

Florence Lake on the Himes Peak Trail.

This recently completed trail takes you on a walk around the north side of Himes Peak. It begins near the Wall Lake Trailhead and leads west up a moderate slope of pine forest and open, marshy meadows. After a one-half mile hike, it turns north to go around the base of the peak, which rises to a height of 11,201 feet. This is a prominent landmark you'll see for some distance along the road on the way to begin your walk.

The grade is moderate as the trail rounds the peak, then turns southwest. As you come closer to the side of the mountain, the path becomes steeper and uses switchbacks to make a short descent. A little farther along, the path flattens, leading onto a long, narrow, open shelf holding picturesque Florence Lake. If you plan to camp, you'll find sites on the level ground west and south of the lake well away from the water. Some reports say there are no fish in the lake but the scenery still makes the walk or horse ride worthwhile.

Past Florence, the trail continues southwest through the timber, where it soon joins Trail 1819 after a one-half mile hike.

TRAPPERS LAKE

The outlet of Trappers Lake.

Not only is Trappers Lake one of the better known landmarks on the Flat Tops, it is also the largest natural body of water in the Wilderness. It has an area of 320 acres and is reported to have a depth of 180 feet. Trappers was created when a wall of ice piled rubble across the north end of the basin, forming a natural dam. It is believed that this occurred at the close of the Wisconsin period, the final episode of glaciation in North America that ended a few thousand years ago. Rock to form the dam came from carving the Chinese Wall and the valleys leading into the basin. The lake is the source of the North Fork of the White River.

Trappers has long been famous for its pure strain of Colorado River cutthroat trout. In spite of the pressure it receives, it's still a good fishery. This is due in part to special regulations for the lake. The use of bait is prohibited. Anglers are restricted to using flies or lures only and all fish over ten inches must be released unharmed. Certain areas of the lake, such as inlet streams and the outlet, are off limits to anglers. This protects the breeding size fish.

In the spring, the cutthroats make spawning runs up the inlet streams around the lake. Colorado Division of Wildlife biologists net the fish as they try to spawn, to collect the eggs for hatchery operations. The cabins you see on the east shore are used by Division personnel during this operation. The Colorado River cutthroat is considered a threatened species and rearing in the Division's hatcheries is one way the species is being protected.

In recent years, brook trout have made their way into Trappers Lake. Because they are so prolific, soon overpopulating a lake or pond, they compete for food with the native cutthroat trout. As such, the Division of Wildlife has no restrictions on brookies other than the method of angling. Fishermen are encouraged to remove all brook trout caught and not return them to the lake.

Because Trappers is within the Wilderness, the use of motorized equipment is prohibited. That doesn't mean you can't get out on the lake, though. Hand propelled boats are allowed, as are belly boats. Trappers Lake Lodge rents rowboats and canoes, which are kept along the northeast shoreline. Make arrangements for rentals at the lodge office. If you're not familiar with the lake or how to fish it, you can hire a guide through the lodge.

Not everyone who visits Trappers comes for the fishing. The scenic beauty alone makes it worth the trip. For the non-angler, there's still an opportunity to watch these colorful trout. The outlet stream is an especially good place to observe them in the evenings as they rise to tiny insects on the surface, or scrounge for nymphs on the bottom of the clear stream.

To help preserve the wilderness environment around the lake, camping is prohibited within one-quarter mile of the shoreline. Campgrounds are provided, though, on the northwest side of Trappers Lake and are accessible by cars, trailers, and RVs.

WALL LAKE TRAIL 1818

Description
The ascent on this trail is deceptive. It's a continuous climb, but the grade is never steep until you get near the headwall of Heberton Creek that feeds into Trappers Lake. You get a very good view of Trappers Lake along the trail as you ascend the valley and again near Wall Lake at a place named the Amphitheatre. Once on top, the trail is nearly flat as it meanders over tundra and through scattered patches of timber.

Destination
Trail 1825, Wall Lake, Trail 1816

Distance
4, 5, 8 miles.

Elevation
9,755 at Trailhead, 11,190 south of Wall Lake.

Directions to trailhead
Seventeen miles east of Buford, go south 7.8 miles on Forest Road 205 to Trappers Lake Lodge. Forest Road 209 goes right across the North Fork of the White River, across from the lodge. It's 1.7 miles from the turnoff to the Wall Lake Trailhead, just past the turn to Scotts Bay Trailhead.

Maps
Big Marvine Peak, Trappers Lake

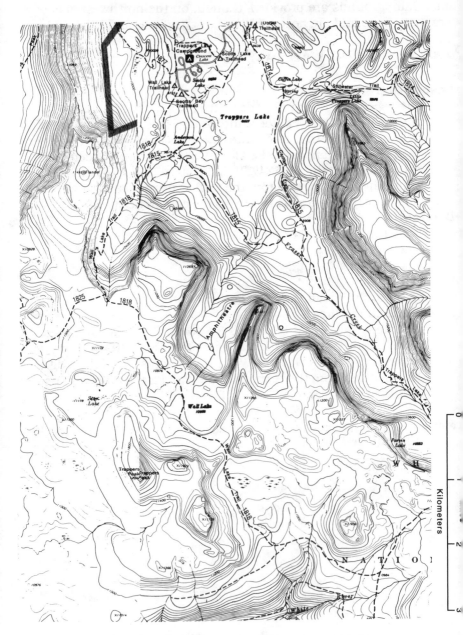

Wall Lake Trail 1818. Map 122, West, 122, East —
Trails Illustrated Topo Map.

Hiking the Wall Lake Trail.

The trail begins on a southwest bearing taking you through stands of tall pines and spruce. On the east side near the path, one-half mile from the trailhead, you'll see two off-colored mosquito hatcheries. Take along some *Deet* and use it liberally, especially early in the season. A little further, you pass Anderson Lake, again on the left. A few yards past the lake, the trail crosses a sloping meadow, where you have your first view of the vertical walls at the top of the valley. About halfway up the trail, you'll have a good view of Trappers Lake, off to the east.

Though it doesn't show on the topos, several snowmelt streams cross the trail, providing adequate water for your hike. About three miles from the trailhead, the ascent begins climbing faster up the side of this cirque carved during the last ice age. Switchbacks make it bearable.

As you approach the top of the valley, look to the left. There, the stream that drains the pothole lakes at the rim plunges over several falls at the headwall, dropping nearly vertically for two hundred feet. It's worth a photo.

The last few feet of your climb take you across the steep, rocky slope of the headwall. Once on top, you can look back down the deep valley and think, "Hey, that wasn't so bad."

As soon as you top out on the plateau, you reach the junction with Trail 1825. Trail 1818 leads to the left, 1825 to the right. The junction is marked only with a post and it is easy to miss the connecting trail, as it's almost obscured by low willows.

Heading southeast toward Wall Lake you pass four unnamed pothole lakes sitting on the open tundra below Trappers Peak. The massive peak rises a thousand feet above the land to an elevation of 12,002. The trail south crosses low rises in the treeless plain. Scattered patches of low willows are the only growth for nearly a mile. The trail along this area is across easily eroded land. Over the years, several parallel paths have created a scar, illustrating graphically the need to stay on established routes.

Wall Lake is 1.5 miles past the canyon rim. It sits out in the open on a flat overlooking a cirque named the Amphitheatre. In the distance across the valley is the Chinese Wall and a section of the plateau that extends for several miles north. Trappers Lake can be seen in the distance. Good campsites can be found in the timber near Wall Lake.

The trail crosses a low, barely discernable pass, Trappers Pass, one-half mile past Wall Lake, the high point on the trail. In the next mile, you descend no more than 100 feet as you cross a large flat covered with the remnants of the ice age. Pothole lakes and marshes cover the area. On the open flat, you connect with a trail that wanders west for a mile above the South Fork Canyon. The main trail works its way around the head of the canyon, where it connects with Trail 1816.

As you approach the trail, you cross several tiny trickles forming the headwaters of the South Fork of the White River, flowing nearly a thousand feet below the soles of your hiking boots.

STILLWATER TRAIL 1814

Description

This one takes you on a steep hike up the Chinese Wall to the top of the plateau, where you connect with other trails. Trail 1120, to the east, takes you into the Bear River drainage and to Stillwater Trailhead.

Destination

Trail 1815, Coffin Lake, Little Trappers Lake, Trail 1803

Distance

1, 1 1/2, 2, 5 miles.

Elevation

9,690 at trailhead, 11,314 at Trail 1803

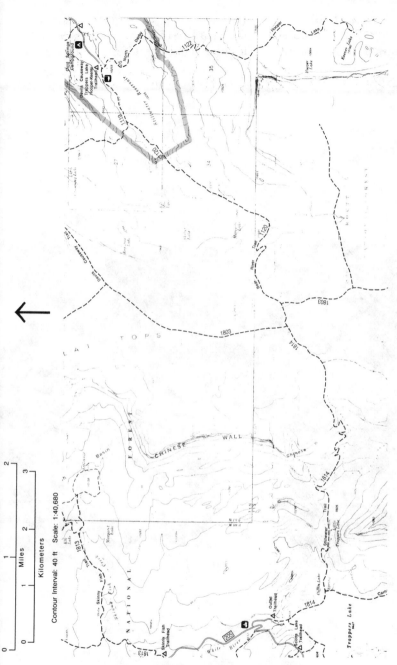

Stillwater Trail 1814, Map 122, East
— **Trails Illustrated Topo Map.**

Directions to trail

From Outlet Trailhead, follow trail 1815 south along east shore-line to DOW cabins. Trail heads east from here.

Maps

Trappers Lake

The Stillwater Trail east of Trappers Lake.

The wall beside the parking lot for the trailhead is a part of the moraine that dammed Trappers Lake. Your hike begins by ascending this low remnant of glacial rubble.

When you reach the outlet of Trappers Lake, continue around the east shoreline. Between the trail and shoreline, you'll see two cabins to the south. They were built about a century ago and the Colorado Division of Wildlife (DOW) now uses them as their base of operations during the spring when cutthroats are spawning. The Trappers Lake cutts supply DOW with most of the spawn used in their hatcheries.

Near the cabins is the junction of Trail 1815, which takes you on a stroll around Trappers Lake. Heading east up Trail 1814 leads past Coffin and Little Trappers Lakes. The climb is noticeable but not strenuous. Coffin Lake sits secluded in a small basin, timbered on one side and the other being a steeply-piled remnant of rubble discarded by a passing glacier. The water appears dark, even lifeless. Don't let that fool you, though, as it's reported that the Division of Wildlife sometimes stocks old brood fish of such a size as to create fish stories.

After leaving Coffin Lake, the trail winds its way up the steep-sided, narrow canyon of the stream draining Little Trappers. The walk is not difficult as the ascent is moderate and steady. Not quite a mile from Coffin, the trail breaks out into the open on a shelf holding Little Trappers Lake. It sits below a steep, timbered hillside that rises more than 1,000 feet to the south. A mile to the east, you have a view of the southern end of the Chinese Wall overlooking the basin. Little Trappers is small and not too deep. Its cutthroats are small, about ten to thirteen inches in length and anxious to take a fly. If you plan to stay overnight, you can find camp sites in the open flat east of the lake or in the wooded area to the north.

Leaving Little Trappers, the trail again climbs, leading across the lower slopes of the Chinese Wall before making the ascent up the seemingly vertical rock face. Switchbacks make the upward hike bearable. After two miles of climbing, you break out on the plateau 1,100 feet above the lake. Another one-half mile takes you to the junction of Trail 1803.

CARHART TRAIL 1815

Description

This trail takes you on a loop trip as it follows the shoreline of Trappers Lake.

Destination

Trail 1816, Trappers Lake Loop, Trail 1818

Distance

5 miles.

Elevation

9,590 at Forest Road 205, 11,275 on the plateau above Fraser Creek at Trail 1816.

Directions to trailhead

Seventeen miles east of Buford, go south eight miles on Forest Road 205, past Trappers Lake Lodge to Outlet Trailhead.

Maps

Trappers Lake (See Page 91)

Division of Wildlife cabins on Trappers Lake.

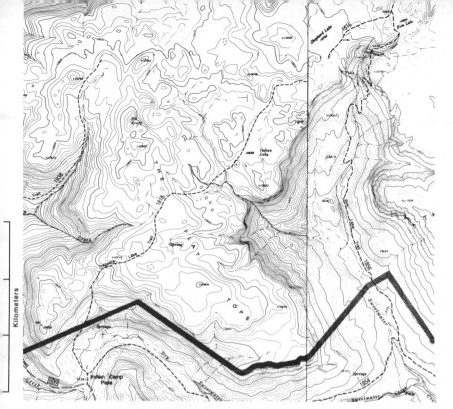

*Trappers Lake Trail 1816. Part 1. Map 122 West &
122 East* —**Trails Illustrated Topo Map.**

Trappers Lake is the crown jewel of the Flat tops Wilderness
Area. Arthur Carhart, for whom this trail is named, believed the
area was too valuable a resource to allow development to occur
here. His dream culminated in the Wilderness Act of 1964, saving
the Flat Tops for future generations. A plaque along the lake trail
honors this visionary conservationist.

Begin at the Outlet Trailhead and walk south along the east
shoreline on Trail 1814. Past the Division of Wildlife cabins, the
trail continues south, taking you over the open shoreline of the
lake. High above you to the southeast lies the Chinese Wall, rising
vertically nearly 2,000 feet and nearly surrounding the lake. A mile
past the junction, the trail wanders away from the shore and heads
into the dense timber a short distance to connect with Trail 1815.

From this junction, the path heads west along the edge of a
meadow to cross Frazer Creek, one of the inlet streams that supplies Trappers. After crossing the creek, the trail climbs a bit through
the trees, where it crosses a stream flowing down through the
Amphitheatre.

The trail turns northeast and leads across a timbered slope
before emerging into a large meadow having several small ponds.

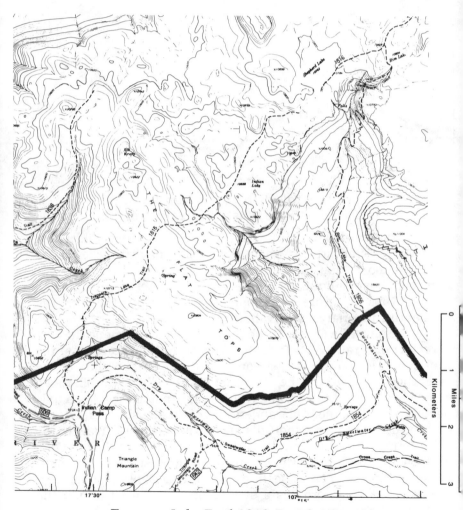

Trappers Lake Trail 1816. Part 2. Map 122
East —**Trails Illustrated Topo Map.**

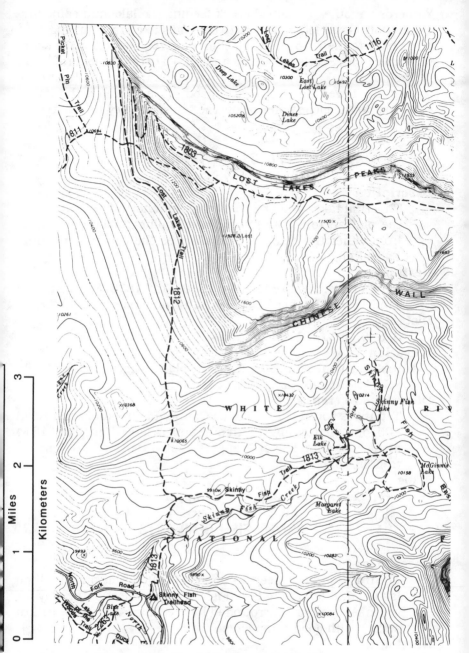

Skinny Fish Trail 1813. Map 122, East
—Trails Illustrated Topo Map.

You cross another unnamed creek feeding the lake and come to a T-junction. Going left takes you to the Wall Lake Trail, turning right leads back to the Trappers Lake shoreline. You can follow the shore to connect with Scotts Lake Trail and return to the Outlet Trailhead. At the north end of Trappers, you will cross the outlet stream. No fishing is allowed here. This is a good place to watch the native cutthroat in the clear water below the bridge as they rise to feed on insects.

TRAPPERS LAKE TRAIL 1816

Description

This trail takes you cross-country from north to south across the plateau to Indian Camp Pass Trailhead. You can hike it from either trailhead. For details, see the description under Eagle Ranger District. Page 185.

Destination

Parvin Lake, Trail 1842, Trail 1818, Trail 1832, Rim Lake and Trail 1856, Shepherd Lake, Indian Lake, Indian Camp Pass.

Distance

3, 5, 6, 9, 11, 12, 14, 16 miles.

Elevation

9,908 at Trail 1815, 11,275 on the plateau above Fraser Creek, 9,724 at Indian Camp Pass.

Directions to trail

Ten miles south of Rio Blanco County Road 8 on Forest Road 205, one-quarter mile north of Trappers Lake. Take Trail 1814 along east shoreline of Trappers Lake, then Trail 1815 south to Trail 1816.

Maps

Deep Lake, Sweetwater Lake, Trappers Lake

SKINNY FISH TRAIL 1813

Description

The trail has a few steep sections in the first mile but the climb isn't bad. It follows Skinny Fish Creek for most of the way. At the lakes, you are surrounded by the Chinese Wall. Beautiful setting with good camp sites.

Destination

Trail 1812, Skinny Fish and McGinnis Lakes

Distance

1, 3 1/2 miles

Elevation

9,235 at trailhead, 10,192 at Skinny Fish Lake

Ron Belak on the Skinny Fish Trail.

Directions to trailhead

Seventeen miles east of Buford, go south 6.7 miles on Forest Road 205. The trailhead is on the east side of the road by Skinny Fish Creek.

Maps

Devils Causeway

From the time you leave the trailhead, you will climb. The first mile is the worst of it, in which you ascend just over 600 feet through an open hillside. You cross Skinny Fish Creek about three-quarters of a mile past the trailhead. A wooden bridge allows hikers to stay dry while crossing the rushing, tumbling thirty-foot wide stream. Horse riders will want to direct their mounts through the water. One-quarter mile past the stream crossing, you come to Trail 1812, which is marked only with a post at the junction. Go right here to stay on Trail 1813.

Past the junction, the trail ascends much more gradually past open grassy meadows. You will often be in sight of Skinny Fish Creek, which has a few beaver ponds. Along the way are several stream crossings, none of which are obstacles. Rocks and logs in the water let you avoid getting your feet wet. One crossing that is a bit boggy has a small wooden bridge over it.

The trail splits 2.5 miles from the trailhead. The left fork continues on to Skinny Fish Lake, the right goes to McGinnis Lake. Skinny Fish is one-half mile farther, McGinnis is about three-quarters of a mile away. Both lakes sit in a large cirque below the Chinese Wall, rising fifteen hundred feet to the north, east and south. The scenery is worth the walk.

Each lake has a path leading around the shoreline. Both have suitable campsites around the lakes.

A small unnamed lake lies one-half mile north of Skinny Fish Lake, feeding the inlet stream. Only a dim path follows the steam, leading over numerous downed trees in your way. The effort is worth it, though. The outlet of the small lake is a cascade over rocks and windblown timber. On the Chinese Wall, depending on the season, you'll see several falls cascading down the steep rock face.

Skinny Fish Lake has been enlarged at some time in the past by an earth-fill dam. East of the dam, about one-quarter mile is a trail, not maintained, connecting to McGinnis Lake, one-quarter mile south. Both lakes have fish, brookies, cutthroats and rainbows.

PICKET PIN TRAIL 1811

Description

Trail 1811 is in two sections; the Picket Pin Trail, which follows Picket Pin Creek, and the Lily Pond Trail, which begins at the bottom of Ripple Creek Pass. The two sections meet beneath the Lost Lakes Peaks, rising to the east. From whichever trailhead you begin, you'll climb a moderately steep grade.

Destination

Trail 1803, Picket Pin Park, Lily Pond Trailhead

Distance

4, 5, 10 miles

Elevation

8,760 at trailhead, 10,684 south of Picket Pin Park, 8,660 at Lily Pond Trailhead

Directions to trailhead

Seventeen miles east of Buford, go south 3.3 miles on Forest Road 205. The trailhead is on the east side of the road by Picket Pin Creek.

Maps

Devils Causeway, Ripple Creek

Picket Pin Park near the junction of the Picket Pin and Chinese Wall

The trail generally follows Picket Pin Creek for the first three miles. In that distance, you ascend about 1,500 feet as you work your way through timber and small parks. The last mile of the climb leads through stands of tall spruce. As the trail tops out, you will see a junction of Trail 1812. At this point, trail 1811 turns sharply to the left and heads north to Picket Park. Going right takes you down Trail 1812, which will connect with the Skinny Fish Trail.

Picket Pin Park is a 1.5-mile-long meadow, trending north-south. Near the south end of the park, you'll see a faint trail heading north. It connects with Trail 1803 and will take you to the trailhead on CR 8, one-quarter mile west of Ripple Creek Pass.

In the park, Trail 1811 turns to the west and begins a gradual drop. You descend through a scattering of timber and smaller meadows. In many of the meadows in this area, you'll find a plant, the false solomanseal, often mistaken for skunk cabbage. This leafy member of the lily family grows in wet, open places, crowding out all other plants and flowers. It blooms in late summer, having blossoms that extend above the leafy part by a foot or so. The flower is white or very pale green. It's not of any particular interest other than its abundance in the areas around this trail and is likely responsible for the name of Lily Pond Park. You'll also find this plant on other Flat Tops trails.

After a mile, the gradient increases as the trail leads to Lily Pond and Lily Pond Park. After crossing the small park, the trail continues west across a mile-long flat before descending again. the path meanders some as it drops faster over the last two miles, coming out on CR 8 at Ripple Creek.

This entire area, though you encounter some climbs, is not difficult walking. It's also good elk country.

ANDERSON RESERVOIR TRAIL

Description
A short walk to a reservoir that has brook trout.
Destination
Anderson Reservoir
Distance
1 1/2 miles
Elevation
8,760, 9,340
Directions to trailhead
Seventeen miles east of Buford, go south 3.3 miles on Forest Road 205. The trailhead is on the east side of the road by Picket Pin Creek.
Maps
Ripple Creek (See Page 112)

The trail begins near the Picket Pin Trail at the parking area but crosses the creek before beginning a short climb. The first one-half mile of the path climbs a short slope, then bends to the left to traverse a slope for one-half mile before swinging northeast. The trail leads through the timber the entire distance until you are near the reservoir, which sits in a small meadow, surrounded by trees on three sides.

Forest Road 8

(County Road 8)
CHINESE WALL TRAIL 1803

Description

The first mile of the trail follows a former road to the Wilderness boundary. It begins as an easy hike with a view of the Lost Lakes Peaks ahead to the south. As the trail nears the peaks, it begins to climb, leading onto the plateau and a view of the entire Flat Tops Wilderness. The route connects with other trails, giving access to the east half of the Wilderness. This is a good trail for a horse ride.

Destination

Trail 1103, Trail 1812, Lost Lakes Peaks, Devils Causeway, Trail 1814, Trail 1120, Trail 1802, Trail 1842

Distance

4, 5, 6, 11, 14, 16, 19 miles

Elevation

10,276 at the trailhead, 11,730 at Lost Lakes Peaks, along the Chinese Wall

Directions to trailhead

On CR 8 about twenty-five miles east of Buford and one-quarter mile west of Ripple Creek Pass. Park by the corral on the south side of the road or in the large parking area across the road to the north.

Maps

Devils Causeway, Ripple Creek, Trappers Lake (See Page 113-115)

*Picket Pin Park near the junction of the
Picket Pin and Chinese Wall trails*

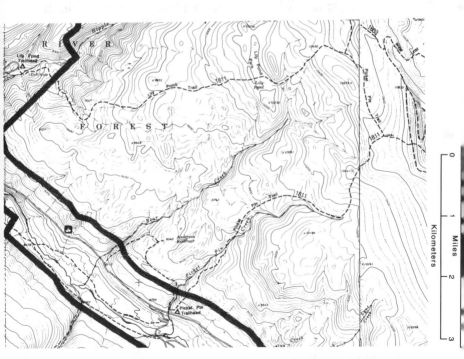

*Picket Pin Trail 1811, and Anderson Reservoir Trail. Map
122 West & 122 East —* **Trails Illustrated Topo Map.**

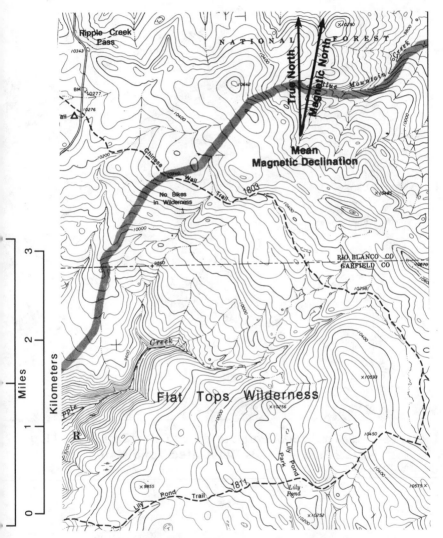

Chinese Wall Trail 1803, Part 1 Map 122 West —
Trails Illustrated Topo Map.

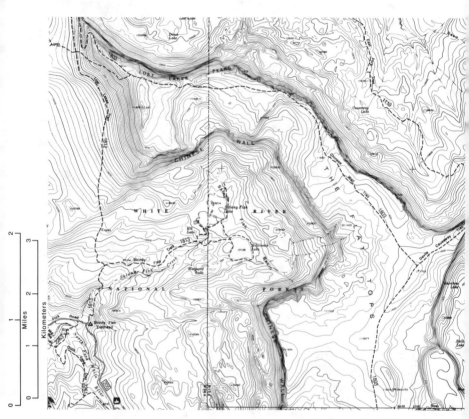

Chinese Wall Trail 1803, Part 2 and Lost Lakes Trail 1812. Map 122 East — **Trails Illustrated Topo Map.**

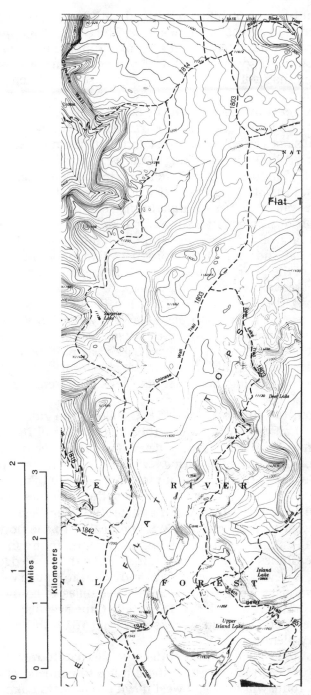

Chinese Wall Trail 1803, Part 3, and Deer LakeTrail 1802.
Map 122 East — Trails Illustrated Topo Map.

You begin your hike on a broad path leading through pine and spruce, and across open meadows. The trail has a few moderate ups and downs. Intermittent streams drain the area, providing a water source in spring and during wet years. The streams form boggy areas that will be sloppy early in the season, forcing you to detour around some of the wettest areas.

You get your first peek at the Lost Lakes Peaks as you enter the opening one-half mile from the trailhead. Actually a ridge-line, the plateau slopes steeply to the west, forming the small peaks reaching to nearly 12,000 feet. Looking to the west, you'll see the plateau above the North Fork of the White River. In the distance, the Little Marvine and Big Marvine Peaks rise above the plateau.

The trail continues meandering in a southerly direction, leading through open woods and broad parks. At 2.5 miles, the trail enters the largest meadow, one and one-half-mile-long Picket Pin Park. Here, abundant moisture produces forage for elk. From the north end of the park, you have a view of the chain of peaks above the Lost Lakes in the basin to the east.

Along the east side of Picket Pin Park, the trail begins a moderate ascent, taking you across a lightly wooded slope to the ridge below the peaks. On top of the ridge, you connect with Trail 1103, which leads east into the Lost Lakes basin. If the Lost Lakes are your destination, this trail is the easiest route, though it is a mile longer than taking the Picket Pin Creek Trail from Forest Road 205.

From the junction, Trail 1803 follows the ridge, heading uphill. One-half mile up the way is the junction of Trail 1812, which leads down to Trail 1813, 3 miles away. Trail 1803 begins climbing more steeply from here, following switchbacks up the steep slope. After a mile, the path emerges into the open. As you hike along the edge of the Lost Lakes Peaks, your view of the wilderness is unimpeded. You look east to Mandall Pass, south to the Devils Causeway, and west to Trappers and Marvine peaks. To the north, you see Pagoda Peak, its form resembling the temples found in Asia.

The Chinese Wall Trail continues along the east edge of the rim, giving a view of the Lost Lakes, and south to Causeway Lake. The trail wanders along the plateau for five miles to connect with the Devils Causeway Trail. See The Devils Causeway listing under SH 131. Between Lost Lakes Peaks and Trail 1814, there's no water, so carry plenty.

Past the Causeway, the trail continues south over the high, nearly featureless plateau three more miles to connect with Trail 1814. This route will take you west down to Trappers Lake.

The path turns east for one-half mile to join Trail 1120, which leads to Stillwater Reservoir. Trail 1803 then heads south again, leading past unnamed potholes as you cross the plateau. Though the trail is high, above 11,000 feet, the walk isn't difficult.

A mile south of Trail 1120 is an undesignated trail heading east for three miles. It crosses the head of the Bear River and leads to the bluffs overlooking Hooper and Keener Lakes.

Trail 1803 connects with Trail 1802 two miles south of the Bear River Trail. The Chinese Wall Trail continues wandering south. At two miles, it begins a descent across a low but steep slope. In this area, it connects with the path leading north to Surprise Lake. South of the junction, Trail 1803 crosses a small flat past a few unnamed lakes. The trail ends at a three-way junction, where it joins Trails 1817 and 1842.

DEER LAKE TRAIL 1802

Description

The trail leaves the plateau and follows a north-south rim above the Middle Fork of Derby Creek. Connects Trails 1803 and 1842.

Destination

Deer Lake, Island Lakes

Distance

1, 3 miles

Elevation

1,590 at Trail 1803, trailhead, 11,480 south of Deer Lake, 11,180 at Trail 1842

Directions to trail

Accessed from Trail 1803, three miles south of Trail 1814, or From Trail 1842 in the Island Lakes area.

Maps

Trappers Lake (only a part of the trail is shown on the USGS quad) (See Page 115)

This trail is incorrectly shown on the 1993 Trails Illustrated Map as 1803, but correctly shown on the White River National Forest Map as 1802.

The trail departs Trail 1803 along the plateau among a group of pothole lakes. After walking east one-half mile, the path heads south, descending across low, steep bluffs on the way to Deer Lake. The lake sits on a small flat overlooking the Middle Fork of Derby Creek to the east. Camping is restricted near the lake. You may camp only in designated sites.

Past Deer Lake, the trail climbs a low but steep slope, then continues in a southerly direction along a broad ledge, making a gradual descent to Trail 1842 and the Island Lakes.

FOREST ROAD 16

(Also County Road 8)

Ripple Creek Pass is the boundary of the White River and Routt National forests. On the east side of this divide, the road designation changes from Forest Road 8 to Forest Road 16. Some maps also show it designated as Rio Blanco County Road 8 until it reaches the Routt County line.

A small, free campground is located at Vaughn Lake on the south, beside the road, four miles east of the pass. Another three miles east takes you to Forest Road 962, which heads to the south. A sign here reads "Trail 1172 Transfer." This road ends a mile away at a gate.

The Pyramid Guard Station is two miles past this road and one mile farther is the trailhead for Trail 1200, leading to Pyramid Peak. Another 2.5 miles takes you to the junction of Forest Road 16 and Rio Blanco County Road 55. Go right or east to stay on Forest Road 16. About ten miles farther east, after crossing Dunkley Pass, a road goes south to Sheriff Reservoir, Forest Road 959. This road gives access to Trail 1117.

The Routt County line is six more miles to the east, where the road becomes Routt County Road 132. After four miles, the road divides. The branch to the left is Routt County Road 15 and takes you to Phippsburg. The right is Routt County Road 17 and goes into Yampa. At both towns, the roads connect with State Highway 131.

Current information on the following trails is available from:

Yampa Ranger District
Routt National Forest
300 Roselawn
PO Box 7
Yampa, CO 80483
(303) 638-4516

TRANSFER TRAIL 1172

Description

This trail saves a mile of walking when taking Trail 1119 south. It follows a former road and is an easy walk.

Destination

Trail 1119, Blue Mountain Creek

Distance

2 miles

Elevation

9,020 at gate, 9,270 at junction to Blue Mountain Creek, 9,066 at Trail 1119

Directions to trailhead

Four miles east of Ripple Creek Pass on County Road 8 (Forest Road 16) to sign, "Trail 1172 Transfer" at Forest Road 967. South on rough road one mile to gate.

Maps

Devils Causeway, Dunkley Pass

This trail is an alternate access point when heading south on Trail 1119. Don't drive your old Pinto down this road to the trailhead unless you don't mind leaving mufflers, bumpers, or other parts along the way. In addition to being rough, it also gets very muddy when it rains.

Past the gate, the trail is a former road. It's an easy walk through open forest and small meadows. You'll probably see deer along this trail, too. A one-mile walk takes you to a fork, the left path leading down to Trail 1119, which is another one-half mile south. The right fork leads to Blue Mountain Creek and follows it upstream to the west. This meandering meadow stream has small cutthroat in it.

EAST FORK TRAIL 1119
(Pyramid Guard Station Trailhead)

Description

This trail provides hikers and horseback riders access to the northeast part of the Wilderness. You'll follow the East Fork of the Williams Fork, a medium size stream that eventually joins the Yampa River. The trail gives access to area lakes and takes you near the Devils Causeway, a unique glacially-formed structure. You can also hike this trail from Stillwater Trailhead.

Destination

Trail 1172, Trail 1116, Trail 1117, Round Lake & Trail 1116, Causeway Lake, Trail 1120, Stillwater Reservoir Trailhead

Distance

2, 4, 6, 8, 10, 12, 14 miles

Elevation

8,415 at Pyramid Guard Station, 11,590 at pass below Devils Causeway, 10,360 at Stillwater Reservoir

Directions to trailhead

Six miles east of Ripple Creek Pass on County Road 8 (Forest Road 16) to Pyramid Guard Station or from SH 131, go east on Routt County Road 17 to County Road 132, then to Rio Blanco

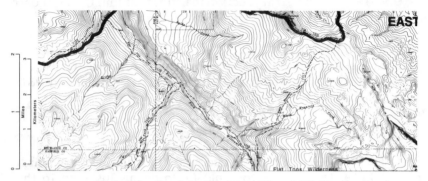

Transfer Trail 1172, Pt 1. Map 122, East
— Trails Illustrated Topo Map.

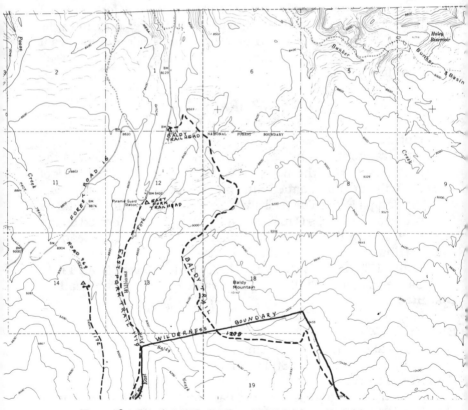

Transfer Trail 1172, Pt 2 —USGS Map, Dunkley Pass

County Road 8 to Pyramid Guard Station. From Yampa, it's about twenty miles to the trailhead. Parking is available across the road from the Guard Station. Rest facilities available.

Maps

Devils Causeway, Dunkley Pass

The East Fork Trail follows the East Fork of the Williams Fork in the valley. Pyramid Peak is seen in the upper right.

The Pyramid Guard Station is neatly hidden in the aspens south of County Road 8. The trail begins here and follows the East Williams Fork, a small creek about fifteen feet in width. Legend has it the stream is named for Old Bill Williams, a scout and trapper who explored Colorado's mountains in the 1830s. The trail stays low, near the stream for the first couple of miles. Baldy Creek joins the Williams Fork from the east where you cross the Wilderness boundary. Here, the trail begins a gentle but steady ascent through the aspen and spruce forest. A mile farther, the trail crosses shallow Blue Mountain Creek, which heads to the west, two miles east of Ripple Creek Pass. Watch for deer and elk in this area.

After crossing Blue Mountain Creek, the trail climbs a bit as it goes around the nose of the ridge, then angles upward across the east-facing timbered slope. Continuing south another one-half mile, Trail 1172 connects from the west. The two paths join at an opening in the timber. The trail follows the contour across the slope, changing little in elevation over the next two miles to connect with Trail 1116.

Past the junction, the trail follows switchbacks down to the East Fork of the Williams Fork and you ford the stream. **The Forest Service advises that this crossing can be dangerous during high water flows.** Above you, to the east, the hillside is an aspen forest. As is expected, the colors in the fall are—well—colorful. Late September and early October finds the region painted in bright yellows, oranges, and deep crimsons in a magnificent luminescence. The next two miles take you through aspen forests and open parks that extend high up the west-facing, steep slopes of 11,532-foot Pyramid Peak. For the next two miles, you follow the Williams Fork upstream along the bottom of the deep valley below the peak. Along this part of the trail, you have a view to the east of the high wall west of Mandall Pass.

The trail ascends the slope east of the stream, where it joins Trail 1117, which heads at Sheriff Reservoir. For the next mile, the trail follows along the stream, taking you south. You cross the creek for the last time, then begin climbing the east-facing slope.

A mile further up the trail, you come to Round Lake. It's a beautiful lake having steep banks on the north side and cutthroats in the water. Just past the lake, you connect with the south end of Trail 1116. A sign marks the junction. The trail crosses the outlet stream from the lake. By staying close to the log-jam dam, you'll find the easiest way across the water.

Sometime around 1900, a forest fire burned much of the valley near Round Lake. Foresters say the land has still not entirely recovered from the lightning-caused fire because of the intense heat that robbed most of the soil's nutrients.

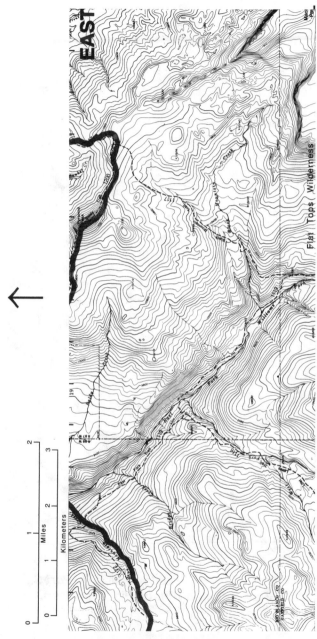

East Fork Trail 1119, Part 1. Map 122,
East — **Trails Illustrated Topo Map.**

123

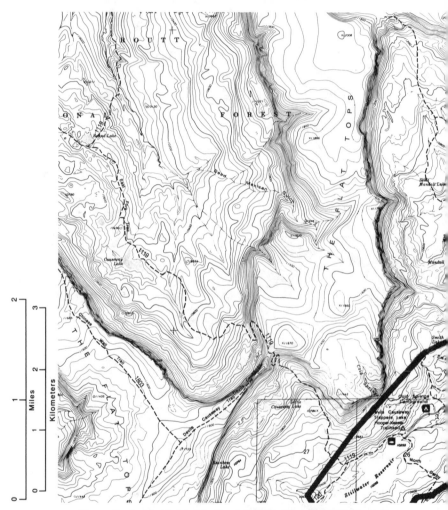

East Fork Trail 1119, and Baldy Trail 1200 Part 2.
Map 122, East — **Trails Illustrated Topo Map.**

Causeway Lake is 1.5 miles past Round Lake, lying in a large open meadow below a nearly vertical, wall several miles long. This section of the trail is an easy walk, having about as much up as down but nothing severe. Looking to the east reveals the steep wall west of Mandall Pass. The largest draw is Dead Mexican Gulch. It acquired its name as a result of an altercation that occurred here many years ago. See the Mandall Lakes Trail for the story.

The trail crosses the outlet of Causeway Lake on logs lying across the small stream. A small pool has formed here below the lake's dam and during spawning runs, is crowded with cutthroat trout. You'll be able to see them easily in the clear water as they move around searching for tasty tidbits floating down to them. Some fish approach sixteen inches in length.

The dam of the lake appears to have been built by beavers. Actually, it's hard to tell if the lake is a large beaver pond, or has just been enlarged by the furry engineers. The lake is shallow and has a grassy shoreline that is quite sloppy to walk through, making it interesting to get close enough to fish.

Good camp sites can be found northwest of the lake, well away from the shoreline. A short distance from the beaver ponds at the west inlet to Causeway, tucked away in the hummocks that have slumped on the unstable slope, several springs emerge from the ground. One is four feet wide where the water pours down a rocky slope. The water is good and it's cold. Refreshing. Almost as good as a beer. It is probably safe to drink without treatment, but be advised there is always a risk when you drink untreated water.

Along the east side of Causeway Lake, the trail leads through the timbered east shoreline, then begins a more rapid, though not steep ascent through smaller stands of timber and meadows. Watch for deer and elk in this area. There are several openings where cow elk and their calves like to graze.

A mile above Causeway Lake, you pass a tiny creek, the last place to get water until you're on the south side of Devils Causeway, a distance of about three miles. Since the ascent will be dehydrating, you may want to fill your canteens here. Be sure to treat the water. Past the creek, the trail climbs steeply to Devils Causeway. The last mile is rocky and a bit loose underfoot. Once on the pass, pause to look around. Back to the north, you'll see Causeway Lake and another lake that is unnamed, sitting on a shelf above and to the south. Because of the pond's location, you won't see it from the valley below. In the distance, you can see a piece of Round Lake, partially hidden in the dense spruce timber.

Across the valley to the south and several miles in the distance sits the broad flat slope of Flat Top Mountain, the highest point in the Wilderness.

Above you to the west is the tip of Devils Causeway, having a path to the top of the ridge. For a description, see the listing under State Highway 131.

At the pass, you can go east up the alpine meadow slope, then head north to Mandall Pass.

Trail 1119 descends the steep walls of a cirque. Switchbacks make the grade easier, but in places, the dirt is loose and footing tricky. Stay on the trail here, as the soils are fragile and easily eroded. After crossing a talus slope, you pass Little Causeway Lake to the west of the trail and a mile below Devils Causeway. Once past the lake, the trail becomes flatter and easier to walk. Near the Wilderness boundary, you pass a shallow, grungy looking pond before connecting with Trail 1120. From here, it's one more mile to the Stillwater Trailhead along the shore of Stillwater Reservoir.

LOST LAKES TRAIL 1116

Description

The trail gives access to the Lost Lakes area from Trail 1119. Fishing is excellent for brookies and cutthroat trout.

Destination

Trail 1103, Lost Lakes, Long Lake, Round Lake

Distance

3, 4, 5, 6 miles

Elevation

9,285 at north junction, 10,720 between East Lost Lake and Long Lake, 10,420 at Round Lake

Directions to trail

Four miles south from Pyramid Guard Station on Trail 1119, or seven miles north on Trail 1119 from Stillwater Reservoir.

Maps

Devils Causeway (See Page 130)

East Lost Lake on the Lost Lakes Trail.

On the nose of a small ridge above a stream named the West Fork, the trail heads uphill to the west from Trail 1119. The trail follows the ridge up through the timber, coming into a meadow after a one-half mile hike. In the clearing, the grade becomes less but still climbs, following the small creek. At the south end of the meadow, the trail wanders away from the stream, following a low ridge above two forks of the West Fork.

After three miles, the trail crosses a low divide and enters a large meadow. Here, you have a view of the Lost Lakes Peaks and the vertical wall that trends southeast above the basin. Immediately below the divide, ahead in the meadow, sits a small, shallow lake known as the Retaining Pond. It's fed by springs saturating the willow covered slopes on the west. South of the pond, the trail connects with Trail 1103, which heads west toward the Lost Lakes Peaks.

Trail 1116 goes south across the small meadow. You encounter a couple of stream crossings. The water is deep. Be careful early in the season. Past the meadow, the trail takes you through the timber. The climb isn't tough but you'll encounter log steps placed across the trail to reduce erosion. Once you get past the steps, about 0.1 mile, you reach East Lost Lake. Its water is clear and deep. The view west is impressive; the glacially carved wall of rock imposes on the basin, diverting attention from everything else.

Continuing on past East Lost Lake, the trail wanders along the steep north bank of the lake, then begins a gentle climb that ends a mile farther, where you cross a low, broad divide. On the downhill side, another mile of hiking takes you to Long Lake. This one is oriented east-west. It's long and narrow and you'll become frustrated at seeing large cutthroats that swim past, ignoring your offerings.

At the west end of the lake, you can walk south a few yards over glacial rubble to three other, smaller lakes. Past Long Lake, it's an easy one-half mile walk to Round Lake.

If you feel ambitious, try getting off the trails in this area. You'll have to pick your way over, around, and sometimes under the randomly stacked downed timber. If you're quiet, though, and observant, you'll have a good chance of seeing elk. If nothing else, you'll at least see an abundance of fresh sign from their passing.

The ground in the area of these lakes is hummocky, rough and uneven. The walk isn't difficult but as a result, really pleasant camp sites are not overly abundant. You'll be able to find sites for a small backpack tent, but expect to look around to find something reasonably level, especially on weekends.

WEST LOST LAKE TRAIL 1103 and 1812

Description
    This trail gives access to lakes below the Lost Lakes Peaks.
Destination
    Deep Lake, West Lost Lake, Trail 1803, Trail 1813
Distance
    1/2, 1, 2, 5 miles
Elevation
    10,080 at Trail 1116, 10,660 at Trail 1803
Directions to trail
    Accessed from Trail 1116, three miles from the junction of Trails 1119 and 1116 along the East Fork of Williams Fork. Also accessed from Trail 1803, four miles south of the trailhead west of Ripple Creek Pass and Trail 1813.
Maps
    Devils Causeway (See Page 130)

*Camp near West Lost Lake. Instead of camping on a lake
shore, wilderness rangers suggest setting up away
from the water to preserve the wilderness.*

This trail leaves Trail 1116 in a large meadow just south of
the Retaining Pond, three miles from Trail 1119. It heads west in
the open before entering the trees and beginning an easy ascent.
The trail makes a bend to the right at a creek crossing one-half mile
from the junction. On the left, you'll see a path leading up a short
hill. It's not marked and is not maintained, but it leads to Deep
Lake, one-quarter mile south.

After stepping across the tiny creek, the main trail resumes
its easy climb. Along the way, you pass a small meadow. During the
spring and early summer, the area can be extremely wet. It's another one-half mile to West Lost Lake, surrounded by dense timber.
Camp sites are limited. To enjoy a quality wilderness experience,
avoid the over-used area beside the trail. Finding other sites in the
trees is difficult because of the uneven ground and downed trees. A
better choice for camping may be the meadow north of the lake and
on the head of the West Fork Creek. It's flat and near water.

At the lake, the trail climbs onto the ridge north of Lost Lakes
Peaks. The ascent is somewhat steep in places but not bad. Once
on the divide, you have a view of the basin to the east, and the
plateau in the distance. Here, the trail connects with Trail 1803.

One-half mile south along Trail 1803, you connect with Trail
1812. It cuts south across a timbered slope to connect with Trail
1813, three miles distant.

129

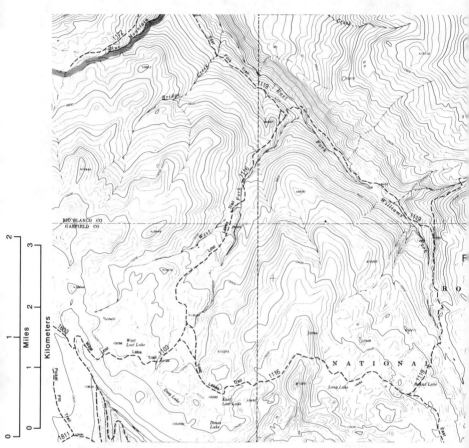

Lost Lakes Trail 1116. Black Mountain Creek Trail and West Lost Lake Trail 1103, Map 122 East — **Trails Illustrated Topo Map.**

BALDY TRAIL 1200

Description

Pyramid Peak is a prominent landmark in the Flat Tops Wilderness. Its distinctive form can be observed from the east along SH 134, more than twenty miles from the peak, and from State Highway 131 as you travel along the eastern edge of the plateau. Trail 1200 takes you on a walk along the peak that sits on the Wilderness boundary.

Destination

Baldy Mountain, Pyramid Peak, Trail 1117

Distance

2 1/2, 5, 7 miles

Elevation

8,264 at trailhead, 11,532 on Pyramid Peak, 11,120 near Trail 1117

Directions to trailhead

On County Road 8 (Forest Road 16) one mile east of Pyramid Guard Station

Maps

Devils Causeway, Dunkley Pass (See Page 124)

Baldy Mountain south of the Pyramid Guard Station trailhead.

Much of the forest along this trail is aspen. Many are old, large trees, in contrast to other parts of the Flat Tops in which spruce are dominant. The first one-half mile of your hike takes you across private property. Stay on the trail to avoid trespassing.

The trail crosses the nose of a ridge, then begins a gentle climb, taking you through willows and up a second ridge. The path winds around, leading through forest, across tiny trickles of water, and across the lower slopes of Baldy Mountain, named for its summit, which is free of timber. At an elevation of 10,142 feet the peak isn't really impressive, appearing as little more than a bump on the landscape. Not all mountains can be fourteeners.

The trail continues its upward route, crossing a slide area before taking you into a meadow at the Wilderness boundary, 3.5 miles from your starting point. You head east through the high open slope on Baldy's south side, then the trail jogs north a short distance to make the rest of the climb easier, avoiding a direct assault on the steep hill north of Pyramid Peak. There are several old sheep trails in this area, which can cause confusion about the route. The trail was reconstructed in 1980, but some problems still exist. Try to follow the most obvious path here.

The main trail continues winding its way southeast, crossing the broad slope through dark pine and spruce forest. A two-mile hike past the Pyramid spur takes you past a boggy area, then on to Trail 1117. Carry water on this hike as the intermittent streams may not be a reliable source to refill canteens.

BLACK MOUNTAIN CREEK TRAIL 1117

Description

From Sheriff Reservoir, the trail follows the wilderness boundary to the Pyramid Peak area, then meanders through meadows and open woodlands to join Trail 1119. The area along the trail is quite primitive, used primarily during hunting seasons.

Destination

Trail 1200, Trail 1119

Distance

3, 5 1/2 miles

Elevation

9,780 at Sheriff Reservoir, 11,100 east of Trail 1200, 9,730 at Trail 1119

Directions to trailhead

From County Road 8 (Forest Road 16), four miles east of Dunkley Pass or eleven miles west of Yampa, go south on Forest Road 959 four miles to west side of Sheriff Reservoir and end of road.

The Black Mountain Trail begins beside Sheriff Reservoir. The Sand Creek Trail ends here.

This is a mystery trail. It's named the Black Mountain Trail and it crosses Black Mountain Creek. So where is Black Mountain? You sure won't find it on any map of this area. Well, give it some thought as you enjoy the hike.

The path heads southwest from Sheriff Reservoir, taking you to the Wilderness boundary, one-half mile away. The trail follows an old logging road for the first mile, through a large meadow for 2.5 miles before entering the Wilderness. Along the way, you climb rather quickly and are soon nearly 1,000 feet above the reservoir, which you'll see to the east. The trail turns south, still ascending, though less abruptly now. The grade begins to flatten, then starts a gentle descent through the timber. You break into a clearing, small at first, that soon opens into a large meadow south of the trail. The high point on the trail gives a view of Pyramid Peak, a mile west. Looking north, you'll see Dunkley Pass and the Dunkley Flat Tops. Sand Point, at 11,182 feet, is also visible to the east. At three miles, you connect with trail 1200.

From here, the trail continues its easy descent, leading through small stands of trees and across open parks, giving you an

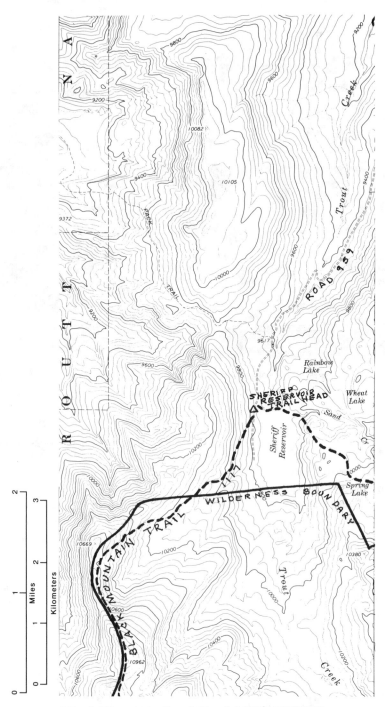

Black Mountain Creek Trail 1117. USGS Maps,
Dunkley Pass, Colo. & Sand Point, Colo.

opportunity to see deer and elk. Those with sharp eyes will often be rewarded. The meadow soon becomes transformed into a low stream valley as you continue downward. The path steepens as you cross Black Mountain Creek, then works its way around a spruce-fir covered ridge. You come into a large, steep hillside clearing as you follow across the slope downhill to connect with Trail 1119.

State Highway 131

Several trails on the east and northeast side of the Flat Tops are accessed from State Highway 131. The good paved highway runs north from the community of Wolcott, just off Interstate 70 north to Steamboat Springs. Along the way the road passes several small ranching and mining communities.

From Interstate 70, exit at Wolcott. From there, it's fifteen miles to State Bridge on the Colorado River, then two more miles to Bond, another wide place in the road. The next town is McCoy, four miles farther north. Less than a mile from McCoy, Eagle County Road 301 heads southwest at the county line. Continuing north, you reach the junction of State Highway 134, the Gore Pass Highway, and the store-gas station at Toponas.

The town of Yampa is another nine miles north. Turning west at the Conoco service station takes you to Routt County Road 7, the road to Stillwater Reservoir. At the north end of town, less then one-half mile farther, going west will get you on county Road 17, which connects to County Road 132, which becomes Rio Blanco County Road 8, taking you to the north side of the Flat Tops.

Going six miles north out of Yampa takes you to Phippsburg. It's four more miles to Oak Creek, another jumping off place for the Flat Tops. Head west on Routt County Road 25, which joins County Road 132. Go west at the junction to connect with Rio Blanco County Road 8.

From Oak Creek, Steamboat Springs is another twenty-two miles north along State Highway 131.

ROUTT COUNTY ROAD 7

Follow Moffat Avenue through Yampa after exiting State Highway 131 by the Conoco station. The street ends at the stop sign in front of the general store. To the left, you'll see a sign indicating Stillwater Reservoir lies to the west along Routt County Road 7. It's about seventeen miles to the reservoir.

Inside the Routt National Forest, the road is designated Forest

Road 900. This road gives access to Coal Creek, Mandall Lakes, Smith Lake, Mosquito Lake, and Hooper and Keener Lakes trails.

Current information on the following trails is available from:

Yampa Ranger District
Routt National Forest
300 Roselawn
PO Box 7
Yampa, CO 80483
(303) 638-4516

SAND CREEK TRAIL 1123

Description
> The trail begins by following a now closed road to the Wilderness boundary. It then follows the boundary, taking you across the Little Flat Tops to Sheriff Reservoir. This is a good place to get away as it is seldom used. A forest ranger said there are lots of elk in the area. You can also hike this trail from Sheriff Reservoir south.

Destination
> Trail 1165, Sheriff Reservoir

Distance
> 4, 7 miles

Elevation
> 10,140 at trailhead, 9,920 at outlet of Sheriff reservoir

Direction to trailhead
> 11.9 miles west of Yampa on County Road 7 and Forest road 900 to Forest Road 906, a rough road requiring a high clearance vehicle, especially if it's muddy. Sign reads Sawtooth Portal. The trailhead is 1.5 miles from the junction.

Maps
> Orno Peak

The Sand Creek Trail.

THE LITTLE FLAT TOPS

The Little Flat Tops is an extension of the Flat Tops Plateau. It's sort of a miniature of the main feature of the Wilderness. The Little Flat Tops is just outside the Wilderness but it's still a roadless area.

Trail 1123 is a road, now closed, that follows East Coal Creek. The route forks one-half mile from the trailhead. The right fork dead ends in another one-half mile, below a peak named Maggies Nipple. Sort of makes you wonder who Maggie was and the story behind the name of the peak?

The left fork of the trail crosses East Coal Creek, then continues north along the bottom of the valley up a gradual ascent. The valley is flat and marshy at the lower end, but the trail stays above the soft goo. The grade is gentle as you continue upstream, to the north, along Coal Creek, named for coal found along its banks. The valley is timbered on the west side but your view up the east side is unimpeded. The bottom flattens out a second time, another boggy area. This time, the trail leads almost through the wetland for a short distance. At the upper end of the bog, you enter a broad meadow at the bottom of gentle slopes on either side, then continue

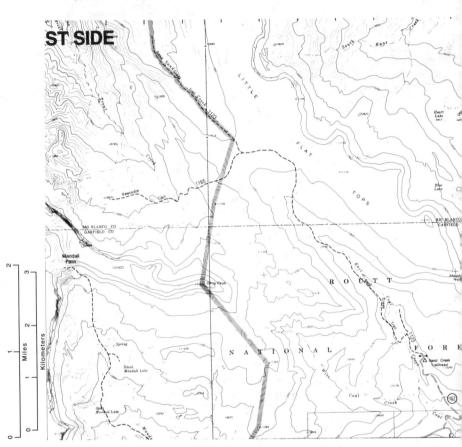

Sand Creek Trail 1123, and Sawtooth Trail 1165
Map 122, East — **Trails Illustrated Topo Map.**

up Coal Creek to near its head before ascending the slope leading onto the Little Flat Tops. As you climb higher up the valley, past the bogs, you have a view of Orno Peak to the west. It's one of the higher peaks on the Flat Tops.

Here, the plateau is broad, having little relief. Directly north lie a few unnamed lakes, one of the sources that feed into Coal Creek. To the south and a bit west, you have a view of Orno Peak, rising to 12,133 feet. The peak sits at the end of a long, narrow ridge, unencumbered by trees. The summit and its steep south-trending slope marks the boundary of the Wilderness. The trail heads west across the flat for nearly a mile, taking you to the Wilderness boundary.

At the edge of the Wilderness, the trail connects with Trail 1165, which heads west. Trail 1123 turns north and begins a barely noticeable descent leading into the Sand Creek drainage. The trail follows the small trickle of water as it travels through the low, broad gully. Continuing north two miles from the trail junction, Sand Creek has eroded the drainage. making it deeper, its sides steeper. The trail crosses Sand Creek and meanders through a willow thicket, now leading down across the steepening slope on the east. Another two miles takes you to a group of small lakes having names like, Crater, Sand, Camel, and Spring. The ground around them is hummocky. You travel northwest another mile, now descending the nose of a broad low ridge where you enter the open at the north end of Sheriff Reservoir.

Along this trail, there aren't any really great camp sites. The trip is long enough, though, that you'll probably want to stay overnight. The best thing to do is to take Trail 1165 west, which crosses several small creeks and ends near a small lake. Camp in this area, then continue the trek north on the second day.

SAWTOOTH TRAIL 1165

Description
This is a good place to get away as the area is seldom used. A forest ranger said there are lots of elk in the area. Once inside the wilderness, the terrain is hummocky as you enter a broad drainage north of 12,133-foot Orno Peak. The trail ends near an unnamed lake in the headwaters of Trout Creek, named for the large cutthroats found here. During the depression of the '30s, local miners panned gold from the stream. The flat ground and scattered timber provide camp sites if you plan to stay overnight here.

Destination
Unnamed lake inside the wilderness

Distance

2 1/2 miles

Elevation

11,040 at junction, 10,960 at end of trail

Directions to trail

Four miles north on trail 1123 from Sand Creek Trailhead.

Maps

Orno Peak (See Page 138)

MANDALL LAKES TRAIL 1121

Description

This route takes you past the Mandall Lakes, all but one good for fishing. Directly north of Black Mandall Lake, you climb to nearly 12,000 feet on Mandall Pass, then can head south over high, rolling tundra. Camp sites can be found in the Mandall Lakes basin, then climb Mandall Pass and return via Stillwater Trailhead for an overnighter.

Destination

Mandall Lakes, Mandall Pass

Distance

4, 5 miles

Elevation

9,840, 11,980

Directions to trailhead

13.9 miles west of Yampa on County Road 7 and Forest Road 900. The trailhead is well marked. Park on the south side of the road beside Yampa Reservoir.

Maps

Devils Causeway, Orno Peak

Black Mandall Lake on the Mandall Pass Trail.

On the way to the trailhead, you drive by Yamcola Reservoir. During construction of the dam, the leg bone of a mastadon was uncovered.

After climbing the first slope, the trail parallels Mandall Creek. You'll wander in and out of the timber and walk through sloping open hillsides as you make your way to the Mandall Lakes. Aspens on the lower slopes make this a colorful walk in the fall. After crossing Mandall Creek, you hike through Englemann spruce and subalpine fir forest. Where the trail follows the stream bottom, the climb is noticeable. The woodlands are broken at times along the way by long, narrow meadows.

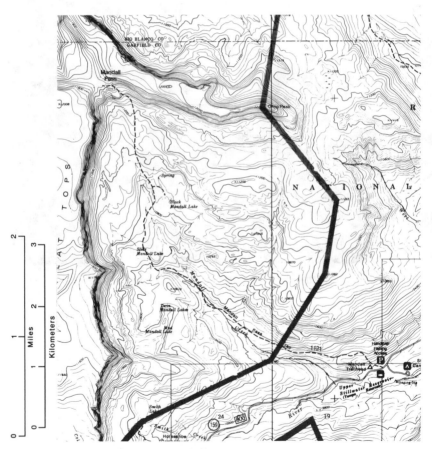

Mandall Lakes Trail 1121. Map 122, East —
Trails Illustrated Topo Map.

After following the drainage 2.5 miles, you arrive at a small shelf that holds four of the five lakes; Mud Mandall, the two Twin Mandall Lakes, and Slide Mandall. Black Mandall is one-half mile farther north. From the small clearings at the lakes, you can see 12,133-foot Orno Peak, two miles to the northeast.

After passing the five Mandall Lakes, you pass several other lakes near the trail that are unnamed. Past these, you enter an alpine meadow as you climb toward Mandall Pass, a mile beyond. The trail climbs rather steeply at the head to the broad glacially-carved valley. Just south of the pass, you almost reach 12,000 feet without even ascending a peak. Even in late summer, you'll often encounter snow here.

There is no trail here, but you can head south over the tundra-like plateau. You will have spectacular views along the way, making the walk worth the effort. Be aware, however, that you may encounter unfavorable weather conditions in a place offering no shelter from the elements. Expect high winds, cool air, bright sun, and changing conditions. Go prepared.

About two miles south of Mandall Pass, along the most narrow section on the flat, you will overlook Dead Mexican Gulch, descending to the west. Eric Petterson, a Forest Service Ranger in the Yampa District, told me how the place acquired its name.

Petterson said one account of the story is recorded in letters to the wife of the Ranger who patrolled the area long before the region was designated as a wilderness. The story varies, depending on the source. In one version, two sheepherders quarreled, the disagreement ending with one murdering the other. The body of the dead sheepherder, who had murdered two people north of Steamboat Springs, fell into a campfire and was burned. His remains were buried in the gulch in 1921. Another version has the Mexican's death occurring as the result of an accident. The grave site is marked on topo and Forest Service maps but is difficult to locate.

Hiking past Mandall Pass over the open land brings you to Devils Causeway a distance of four miles. There is no trail but you should have no problem navigating across the open alpine plateau. Carry plenty of water as none is available after leaving the Mandall Lakes until you reach Little Causeway Lake, a distance of nearly seven miles.

Going north here, you can descend to Causeway Lake and continue on to Pyramid GS. By following Trail 1119 south, you can return to your starting point by way of Stillwater Trailhead and Forest Road 900 to the Mandall Lakes Trailhead.

SMITH LAKE TRAIL

Description
A short, easy hike
Destination
Smith Lake
Distance
0.6 miles
Elevation
10,240, 10,507
Directions to trailhead
16.7 miles west of Yampa on County Road 7 and Forest Road 900, just past Horseshoe Campground. The trailhead is marked. Park along the road
Maps
Orno Peak

The trail crosses Cold Springs Creek, then enters a lightly timbered spruce and fir forest as it heads north to Smith Lake. The hike is short and the trail an easy climb. The Wilderness boundary lies along the south shoreline. The shallow lake, surrounded by trees, reportedly holds cutthroat trout, some of good size. Lower Smith Lake is about 200 yards south of Smith Lake. It is reported to have small cutts. Camping is prohibited within one-quarter mile of the lake.

The lake and creek are named for Tom Smith, a trapper who lived in the surrounding mountains about 1880. One story told of him says he crawled into the den of a grizzly bear, shot it, and sold the fat for ten cents a pound.

Cold Springs Creek earned its name because of its very cold water. Even in summer, temperature of the creek averages 35 degrees.

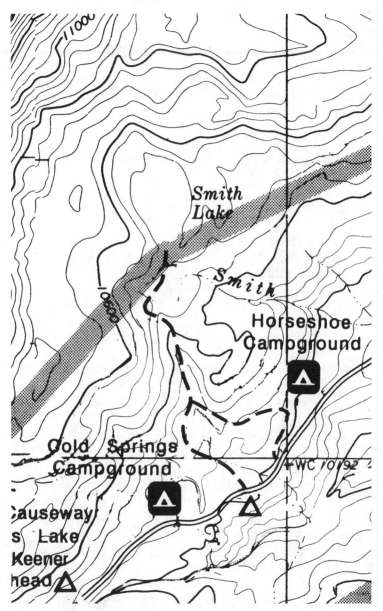

Smith Lake Trail. Map 122 East —
Trails Illustrated Topo Map.

EAST FORK TRAIL 1119
(Bear River Trailhead)

Description

The trail gives access to area lakes and takes you onto the Devils Causeway, a unique glacially-formed structure. You'll follow the East Fork of the Williams Fork north, a small stream that eventually joins the Yampa River. You can hike this trail from the Pyramid Guard Station as well.

Destination

Trail 1120, Devils Causeway, Causeway Lake, Trail 1116 & Round Lake, Trail 1117, Trail 1116, Trail 1172, Pyramid Guard Station

Distance

1, 3, 5 1/2, 7, 9, 11, 14 miles

Elevation

10,360 at Stillwater Reservoir, 11,590 at pass below Devils Causeway, 8,415 at Pyramid Guard Station

Directions to trailhead

From Yampa, go west on Routt County Road 7 to Stillwater Reservoir, seventeen miles.

Maps

Devils Causeway, Dunkley Pass (See Pages 123, 124)

For trail description, see Pyramid Guard Station Trailhead.

DEVILS CAUSEWAY

The Devils Causeway is a unique geologic structure in the Flat Tops Wilderness. The area was created by fire and ice. Lava covered the region to a great thickness, which was later carved into valleys by glaciers. At the Causeway, the glacier nearly succeeded in wearing away the basalt, leaving only a high, thin wall, rising vertically more than 1,000 feet above two drainages. At one point, the wall is narrow—very narrow—no more than four feet in width.

At that point, the Causeway is a jumble of broken rock. Footing is tricky getting across the knife-like ridge. And while the view is spectacular and the feeling one can enjoy while standing above two rugged vistas is exhilarating, it's not a place for those having a fear of heights. The actual danger, though, is more perceived than real.

To reach the Devils Causeway, park at the trailhead at Stillwater Reservoir. (For directions, see Trail 1120). Take Trail 1119 along the north shoreline of the reservoir. Go right at the trail junction, ascending to the Causeway, three miles from the trailhead. A well-used path leads up the steep slope to the west, taking you to one of the more magnificent vistas in the Wilderness. From the ridge, you have unobstructed views in all directions. You'll see several of the many peaks, including Flat Top Mountain to the south, the highest point in the Wilderness. To the northwest, you can observe the highest point along the ridge, the Lost Lakes Peaks. Look southwest into the Bear River valley to see a series of lakes below the Causeway, tucked away among the trees. Above them, the ridge broadens to a width of three or four miles. To the west, Big Marvine Peak rises from the plateau, as do the three smaller Little Marvine Peaks some distance north. In addition to the peaks and high plateau, you'll be fascinated by the many lakes seen from this vantage point.

The Causeway is a popular day hike, perhaps too popular. The last one-half mile, which is above timberline, leads through fragile, easily eroded terrain. Careless hikers have damaged portions of the slope by short-cutting switchbacks. Because of the short growing season at this altitude (above 11,000 feet), restoration of native vegetation is a slow process. Unless hikers stay on the maintained trail, rangers may be forced to close the area to prevent further damage.

BEAR RIVER TRAIL 1120

Description

This trail wanders westward through spruce forest past Mosquito Lake before climbing the headwall onto the plateau. At the junction of Trail 1803, on the plateau, is the White River-Routt National Forest boundary. You can continue west to connect with Trail 1814 and descend to Trappers Lake.

Destination

Trail 1119, Mosquito Lake, Trail 1803

Distance

1, 2.5, 5 miles

Elevation

10,280, 11,412

Directions to trailhead

17.4 miles west of Yampa on County Road 7 and Forest Road 900 at Stillwater Reservoir. Parking is available at the end of the road. Follow Trail 1119 one mile west to junction of Trail 1120.

Maps

Devils Causeway, Orno Peak, Trappers Lake

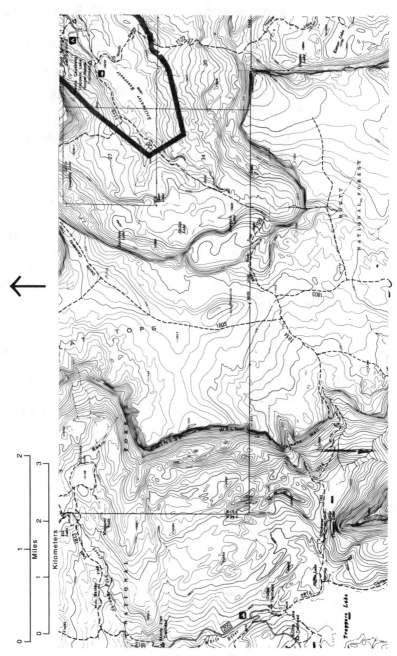

Bear River Trail 1120, Map 122 East
— Trails Illustrated Topo Map.

The Bear River Trail follows the valley, giving access to Mosquito and Skillet Lakes.

The first mile of the trail takes you along the north shoreline of Stillwater Reservoir. The lake was constructed during the 1930s to supply irrigation water to the area ranches. It gets its name from the narrow gorge which once held the flow of several streams forming an area of still water.

You connect with Trail 1119 after one mile. Heading west, you enter spruce and fir forest as you follow the Bear River upstream. The river was given its name by early fur trappers. You pass Mosquito Lake 1.5 miles west, past the junction, which shares a large flat with three other lakes; Skillet, Steer, and Rainbow. No designated trails lead to the lakes but you will be able to follow clearly defined paths to each. You will help to preserve the wilderness experience for yourself and others if you avoid camping close to the lakes.

Past Mosquito Lake, the trail continues generally to the southwest, following Bear River upstream another one-half mile, then bears right to ascend the glacially carved wall that extends south from Devils Causeway. Switchbacks make the climb easier. Once you're on the flat, you'll enjoy spectacular views of the plateau and its many peaks. From the top, it's only one-quarter mile west to Trail 1803 at the White River-Routt National Forest boundary. At the junction, you have several options: continue west to Trappers Lake on Trail 1814, follow Trail 1803 along the Chinese Wall, or hike south to connect with other trails.

Current information on the following trails is available from:

Eagle Ranger District
White River National Forest
125 W. 5th St.
PO Box 720
Eagle, CO 81631
(303) 328-6388

NORTH DERBY TRAIL 1122

(Yampa Ranger District, Routt National Forest)
and
HOOPER LAKE TRAIL 1860
(Eagle Ranger District, White River National Forest)

Description

In addition to giving access to the head of the Derby Creek drainage, North Derby Trail takes you near Flat Top Mountain, the highest point in the Flat Tops Wilderness. Trail 1860 is included here because the Stillwater Trailhead is more easily accessible than the Stump Park Trailhead, from which Trail 1860 may also be accessed. The Derby Creek-Bear River divide, two miles south of Stillwater Reservoir, is the boundary of the two Ranger Districts and National Forests.

Destination
Trail 1860, Hooper and Keener Lakes, Edge Lake Trail, Trail 1859, Trail 1842, Stump Park Trailhead
Distance
2, 2 1/2, 3 1/2, 5 1/2, 6, 9 miles
Elevation
10,280, 11,200 on the divide, 10,800 near Hooper and Keener Lakes
Directions to trailhead
17.4 miles west of Yampa on County Road 7 and Forest Road 900 to Stillwater Reservoir. Parking is available at the end of the road.
Maps
Dome Peak, Orno Peak

Kip Wilson takes a break on the Hooper Lake Trail.

Cross the dam, going south to the junction one-half mile from the parking area. A sign marks the junction. The left fork is Trail 1122. The other follows the south shoreline of Stillwater Reservoir and connects with Trail 1120 west of the inlet.

Past the sign, Trail 1122 begins climbing through spruce and fir forest toward the divide two miles away and nearly 1,000 feet higher, which is the boundary between Routt and White River National Forests. Along the way, you pass through a section burned in 1979. The fire was started by a careless smoker. At the divide, the designation changes to Trail 1860. This divide separates the Colorado and Yampa river drainages.

After crossing the dam, you cross a flat wetland before entering the timber to begin an ascent that will take you above timberline. In places, the climb is rather steep, even on the switchbacks. You pass several small ponds and a trickle of water running downhill, all near the trail and sources of drinking water. Be sure to treat the water. The last one-half mile of the climb is on a steep, rocky path. Footing can be tricky on the loose sand.

Views from the divide are overwhelming. To the north, you see the Devils Causeway, the long, northeast-southwest ridge jutting out from the plateau. Look east from the crest of the divide separating the two National Forests. In the distance to the south, you will see the sharp peaks of the Maroon Bells Wilderness, south

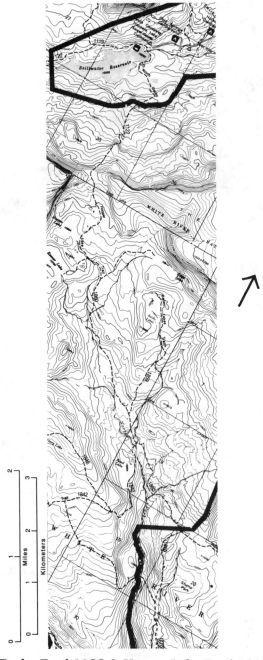

North Derby Trail 1122 & Hooper Lake Trail 1860. Also
Edge Lake Trail and Bailey Lakes Trail 1859. Map
122 East — **Trails Illustrated Topo Map.**

of Interstate 70. There, two miles to the east, you see Flat Top Mountain, the tallest peak in the Flat Tops Wilderness at 12,354 feet. If you're that ambitious, hike to the summit, which is marked by a large pile of rocks. The view will be worth it. On a clear day, visibility exceeds 100 miles.

South of the divide, you cross a grassy knoll to descend into a basin filled with lakes and drained by small streams, the headwaters of Derby Creek. On the west is a high vertical basalt wall, rising to a high knob of 12,186 foot Derby Peak. You'll see a waterfall—depending on the season and amount of remaining snowpack—dropping a few hundred feet off the top, north of the peak.

You come to a fork in the trail, marked only by a small pile of rocks, one-half mile down the slope. The barely noticeable junction is near a small pond just west of the trail. The west fork passes near the outlet of Hooper Lake and can be seen over a low rise. It sits in a bowl below the wall. Keener Lake, the third in a group of four lakes, one-quarter mile farther south, is where you connect with a junction of the trail leading to it. No signs mark the junctions.

Camping is prohibited within one-quarter mile of both Hooper and Keener Lakes. There are meadows nearby, but cattle grazing in the area can make it a challenge to find a pleasant location. The lakes are the best water source, but you should filter or boil it before drinking.

At the first junction after crossing the knoll, the one mentioned above, the left fork of the trail continues down a grassy slope. In places, the trail fades and is hard to find since it isn't maintained. Just stay in the open between the trees along the west and east sides of the meadow. Be aware that cattle may graze the area, so watch where you step. After descending a short slope, the left fork meets the main trail again at the head of a second large, flat meadow.

Hiking another one-quarter mile, you come to a junction with a trail bearing to the northeast, leading to Edge Lake, one mile distant. The junction is marked with a post and the trail is undesignated.

Continuing south on Trail 1860, you cross the one-half mile long meadow, then begin another gradual descent, following the outlet streams from Edge, Hooper, and Keener Lakes. From the Edge Lake trail continue south almost two miles to Trail 1859. This one heads north uphill for two miles, leading to the two Bailey Lakes. Campers staying at Bailey Lakes or Edge Lake must observe the 100-foot restriction.

Another one-half mile past Trail 1859, you connect with Trail 1842. Trail 1860 continues its descent, passing a few unnamed lakes on the way to the wilderness boundary and Stump Park, a distance of two more miles.

153

EDGE LAKE TRAIL

Description

Edge Lake is a long, narrow body of water resting at the bottom of a steep wall 1.5 mile southwest of Flat Top Mountain. The path leaves Trail 1860 at the north end of a large, flat meadow. It heads northeast, wandering around the nose of a timbered ridge, then follows the outlet stream through a second meadow to the lake. You'll find camp sites west and south of the lake. The USGS Dome Peak quad shows a trail between Edge and Bailey Lakes but it's not maintained.

Destination

Edge Lake

Distance

1 mile

Elevation

10,680 at Trail 1860, 10,910 at Edge Lake

Directions to trail

Four miles from Stillwater Reservoir along Trails 1122 and 1860. Also accessed by more difficult route from Forest Road 610 at Stump Park. The distance is about the same as walking in from Stillwater Trailhead, provided you have a high clearance four-wheel-drive vehicle to access the Stump Park Trailhead.

Maps

Dome Peak (See Page 152)

BAILEY LAKES TRAIL 1859

Description

The path departs from Trail 1860 beside a marshy area and heads north. It follows a moderate slope through the trees a short distance before entering a broad, nearly flat meadow, marshy in spots. The trail crosses the outlet from Bailey Lakes, then follows the creek across an almost but not quite flat woodland. You enter another clearing at the lower lake. You'll see the trail leading through the narrow meadow, which leads to the upper lake. You could also follow the stream to the west between the two lakes. The land around the lakes is reasonably flat, providing for camp sites.

The outlet stream, a mile south of Bailey Lakes, is joined by a second small creek entering from the east. In a meadow, hidden by timber, are several ponds that could make for a more secluded camp site.

Destination
　Bailey Lakes
Distance
　2 miles
Elevation
　10,310 at Trail 1860, 10,798 at Bailey Lakes
Directions to trail
　Six miles from Stillwater Reservoir along Trails 1122 and 1860.
　Also accessed by more difficult route from Forest Road 610 at
　Stump Park. This route will shorten your walk by two miles
　provided you have a high clearance four-wheel-drive vehicle.

Dome Peak (See Page 152)

Eagle County Road 301

　　Eagle County Road 301 turns off to the southwest from State
Highway 131, seventeen miles south of Yampa and twenty-two miles
north of Wolcott. The turn is at the county line and is marked with
a sign reading "Burns." After a mile, the road joins the Colorado
River, which it follows all the way to Interstate 70, a distance of
thirty-six miles. The Burns Post Office, on the south side of the
gravel road, is twelve miles down-river. Just past the Post Office,
Eagle County Road 39, also known as the Derby Mesa Loop, heads
northwest.
　　County Road 39 takes you to Derby Junction and the other
end of the Derby Mesa Loop, one mile past Burns. From there, it's
another fifteen miles to County Road 40, the Sweetwater Lake Road.
The next road, 5.5 miles to the south at Deep Creek, is County
Road 17, which becomes Forest Road 600 inside the National Forest boundary. Another 1.5 miles along County Road 301 takes you
to Interstate 70. The lower half of County Road 301 is paved.

EAGLE COUNTY ROAD 39

　　Just past the Burns Post Office, Eagle County Road 39, also
known as the Derby Mesa Loop, heads northwest. Seven miles from
Burns, it connects with Forest Road 610. The junction is marked
with a sign, "Stump Park Road No. 610."
　　Drive 2.5 miles farther along the loop to Forest Road 613,
then five miles to Derby Junction and Eagle County Road 301. The

last two miles of the loop is steep and winding, giving a great view of the Colorado River below.

FOREST ROAD 610

Eagle County Road connects with Forest Road 610, seven miles from Burns. (See above). The first one-half mile is through private property so you must stay on the road. After passing through a gate, you're on public land. Park here unless you are driving a high clearance four-wheel-drive, which is required past the gate to the Stump Park Trailhead.

Current information on the following trails is available from:

Eagle Ranger District
White River National Forest
125 W. 5th St.
PO Box 720
Eagle, CO 81631
(303) 328-6388

HOOPER LAKE TRAIL 1860

Description
This trail connects with Trail 1122, which is described under trails accessed from Routt County Road 7. Reaching the trail head from Eagle County Road 301 requires four-wheel-drive.
Destination
Trail 1842, Trail 1859, Edge Lake Trail, Trail 1120
Distance
2, 3, 5, 6 miles
Elevation
10,200, 11,190
Directions to trailhead
From Eagle County Road 39, go west on Forest Road 610, four miles to junction of Forest Road 612. Go right, staying on Forest Road 610. From the junction, it's three miles to Trail 1860. Because of short but steep grades, a short wheelbase vehicle will handle the road best. The last mile of road goes through volcanic clay soils, which become extremely greasy with even a light rain. It may be best to stay off this portion of the road when it's wet.
Maps
Dome Peak, Orno Peak (See Page 152)

For trail description, see Trail 1120 and 1860 under Yampa Ranger District.

ISLAND LAKE TRAIL 1842

Description

This trail gives you a view of three peaks, Dome and Derby Peaks, and Sheep Mountain. It leads across volcanic debris and soils left behind after the glaciers melted. You'll encounter a lot of small ups and downs on this east-west oriented trail. Clay soils will be especially sticky when wet.

The trail connects Trails 1860 on the east and 1816 on the west.

Destination

Trail 1846, Trail 1858, Trail 1802, Trail 1857, Trail 1817, Trail 1803, Trail 1816

Distance

1 1/2, 4 1/2, 7, 8, 9

Elevation

10,120 at Trail 1860, 11,545 at Trail 1817, 11,275 at Trail 1816

Direction to trail

From Eagle County Road 39, go west on Forest Road 610 four miles to junction of Forest Road 612. Go right, staying on Forest Road 610 to Stump Park Trailhead. From here, you can take Trail 1860 north for three miles. An alternate approach is Trail 1846 to the west. This way, it's two miles to Trail 1842 and you join it two miles west of its junction with Trail 1860.

Maps

Dome Peak, Orno Peak

From Trail 1860, Trail 1842 wanders south past Road Lake for a mile before turning west. At two miles, it connects with Trail 1846, which leads to Solitary Lake. In this distance, the terrain varies, taking you across the flat beside Road Lake, then following the nose of a low, broad ridge through the timber. You exit the trees and ascend a short, steep slope before heading across a large meadow, following the contour. You come to the second part of Trail 1846 one-half mile farther west, which enters from Stump Park.

Past this junction, you hike through stands of timber protruding into the meadows. You cross several creeks. Two miles west of the junction, you come to short spur trails leading to Mud Lake, then Muskrat Lake, both a very short walk to the north. While these are the only lakes here that are named, there are others nearby, both north and south of the trail. You come to Mirror Lake, a long,

*Lower Island Lake seen from near Shingle Peak. Turret Peak
is between the Turret Creek and Shingle Peak trails.*

narrow pond tucked away in a small meadow, one-half mile past
Muskrat Lake. It's another one-half mile from there to the junction
of Trail 1858, which connects from the south after following the
Middle Fork of Derby Creek upstream.

You cross a low, nearly flat meadow as you pass the Middle
Fork and begin a slight upgrade along the outlet from Island Lake.
The trail takes you through stands of pine and spruce as you follow
the gentle rise for two miles to the lake.

Island Lake, the larger of a group of eight lakes, lies on a
shelf, surrounded on three sides by forest. The trail passes along
the northwest shoreline, heading west to ascend a short but steep
slope. The flats east and south of the lake will offer the most
promising camp sites.

After climbing above the lake, you come to a second level,
another ledge holding the other seven lakes. The trail joins Trail
1857, which ascends the steep slope from Mackinaw Lake. Upper
Island sits to the south, 0.1 mile from Trail 1842. The lake is in the
open, unprotected from wind and rain.

Here, the trail also connects with Trail 1802, which leads
north to Deer Lake. One-half mile west, Trail 1842 makes another
short, steep ascent, taking you onto the main Flat Tops plateau.
You skirt the edge of a low willow patch on the south side of a broad

hill rising a bit over 200 feet above you. Another one-half mile takes you to Trail 1817, heading south to W Mountain. A few feet farther, Trail 1842 turns north, leading across a broad flat of short grass, gently sloping to the west. After a mile, you connect with Trail 1803 to continue north. Trail 1842, though turns west, ending at Trail 1816 one-half mile farther. From here, you can go north to Trappers Lake or south to Indian Camp Pass Trailhead.

SOLITARY LAKE TRAIL 1846

Description

This trail is the left fork at the trailhead, leading west. It climbs quickly in the first mile before levelling out a bit. It continues climbing but less abruptly as it crosses an open slope. Two miles from the trailhead, it connects with Trail 1842. Go east here one-half mile to pick up the rest of Trail 1846. At the junction, the trail leads northwest up a broad, gently sloping ridge. The way is through open meadow, broken occasionally by small stands of timber. Solitary Lake sits alone on a small shelf at the end of your hike. On the wall to the west, you'll see Derby Peak, rising to 12,186 feet and the high point of the plateau above you. The best camp sites will be found near the timber south of the lake.

Destination

Trail 1842, Solitary Lake

Distance

2 1/2, 5 miles

Elevation

9,880 at trailhead, 10,638 at Solitary Lake

Directions to trailhead

From Eagle County Road 39, go west on Forest Road 610 four miles to junction of Forest Road 612. Go right, staying on Forest Road 610. From the junction, it's three miles to Trail 1860. Because of short but steep grades, a short wheelbase vehicle will handle the road best. The last mile of road goes through volcanic clay soils, which become extremely greasy with even a light rain. It may be best to stay off this portion of the road when it's wet.

Maps

Dome Peak

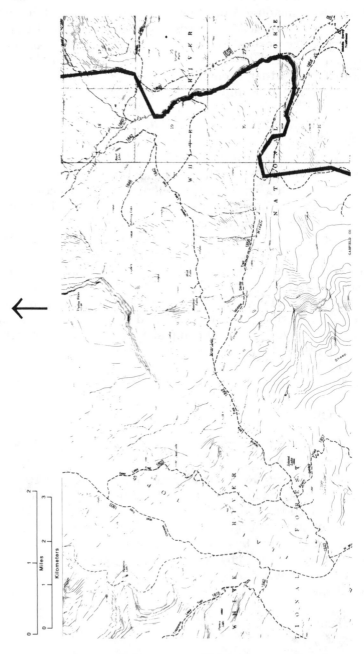

*Island Lake Trail 1842, Middle Derby Trail 1858
and Solitary Lake Trail 1846 Map 122, East —*
Trails Illustrated Topo Map.

MIDDLE DERBY TRAIL 1858

Description

The trail generally follows the Middle Fork of Derby Creek. The ascent is a gradual, not too difficult hike.

Destination

Trail 1836, McMillan Lake, Trail 2076, Trail 1842

Distance

1/2, 2, 2 1/2, 5 1/2 miles

Elevation

8,800 at trailhead, 10,103 at Trail 1842

Directions to trailhead

From Eagle County Road 39, go west on Forest Road 610 four miles to junction of Forest Road 612. Go left. From the junction, it's one rough mile to Trail 1858. Same conditions as Forest Road 610.

Maps

Dome Peak, Trappers Lake (See Page 160)

The trail begins by following the Middle Fork of Derby Creek on the way to McMillan Lake. You connect with Trail 1836 one-half mile from the trailhead, which leads south. It's another 1.5 miles to McMillan Lake and the Wilderness boundary.

The path continues west through timber. Since the trail follows the drainage, the hike is pleasant, not a heart-attack inducing climb. Trail 2076 joins from the south one-half mile past the lake. A few feet farther, the trail bends north to cross Derby Creek before continuing its westward direction. After crossing the creek, the trail takes you across open slopes for a mile before walking through a timbered hillside.

As you continue west along Derby Creek, you come to Trail 2076 a mile past the lake. The gradual climb continues, leading you through a small canyon, wooded on the south side and bare on the north. Three miles past the trail junction, you connect with Trail 1842. As you get closer to 1842, notice the moraines along the sides of the stream valley. These are the elongated piles of rubble left behind when the glaciers receded as they melted.

FOREST ROAD 613

The Derby Mesa Loop connects with Forest Road 613, 9.5 miles from Burns. Turn west, through the gate. The first 1.5 miles is quite rough as it wanders across sandstone, which resists weathering. The road takes you through an area burned in late June 1980. The Emerald Lake Fire destroyed more than 10,000 acres. More than 500 firefighters worked to put out Colorado's biggest forest fire. Smoke was visible as far away as Nebraska. Many standing dead trees remain in the burn area. It has since grown up in aspen. On the trip out, the view to the east is great. You have a view of the mountains all the way to the Continental Divide.

The next section, which takes you to the South Fork of Derby Creek, goes over limestone in the Morrison Formation and is not quite so rough. Past Deer Park, a long, narrow meadow, the road is rough but not real bad. Past the junction with Forest Road 616, you descend into the South Fork of Derby Creek. Ahead to the west, you see Sheep Mountain and its 12,241-foot summit.

Then, you descend a steep, loose, rocky, rough, and bumpy road.

At the bottom, you must ford the South Fork. The crossing is good and solid but the approach is steep leading into the water. A high clearance four-wheel-drive is required, preferably one with a short wheelbase. From here, the road gets bad.

The road is nothing more than tracks through the volcanic debris and clay soils. As long as it's dry, travel is only slow-going. The challenge comes when it rains and the ground turns to slime, offering little traction.

This road is extremely popular with local four-wheel-drive enthusiasts and horse users. There is a trailhead just off the Derby Road for those who want to hike from there. Be aware that the road leads through a very narrow corridor surrounded by Wilderness and off-road travel is prohibited. The road ends at Mackinaw Lake. From there, travel into the Wilderness is by foot or pack animal only.

You may wonder if the drive to Mackinaw Lake is worth the effort. That depends. It will save several miles of walking if the Island Lakes are your destination.

HIKING THE SOUTHEAST FLAT TOPS

The southeast side of the plateau, between Middle Derby and Sweetwater creeks, is one of the more challenging areas for the hiker and backpacker. Here, the volcanoes and glaciers worked overtime to create narrow, steep-sided, deep canyons. Streams draining the plateau did their part, too, deepening the gorges.

The area has some of the more spectacular exposures of the rocks that accumulated over the eons. At the bottom of Sweetwater Creek, rock more than 500 million years old is exposed. The rim above the creek, the light-colored vertical walls, are limestones deposited at the bottom of the shallow sea that covered the region 250 million years ago.

While all this makes for impressive scenery, it also makes hikers work harder to reach the plateau. Ascents on several trails exceed 3,000 feet. As if that's not enough, the gradients are high. The bad news is you must stop often to catch your breath. There's good news, though. The climb is over quickly.

Sheep Mountain above the Crescent Lake Road. The Roberts Trail crosses at the lower end of the ridge to the left of the peak.

ROBERTS TRAIL 2076

Description

A short hike that follows the Wilderness boundary north to Trail 1858

Destination

Trail 1858

Distance

3 miles

Elevation

9,460, 10,100

Directions to trailhead

From Eagle County Road 39, go west on Forest Road 613, eight miles to the trail. four-wheel-drive is needed.

Maps

Dome Peak

This trail provides another way into the Wilderness in the Middle Fork of Derby Creek area. The three-mile hike takes you to Trail 1858. Your walk through the trees is an easy climb.

Midway along the trail is a spur leading to the west and the base of Sheep Mountain. This trail ends at a small pothole. Should you want to ascend the peak, you'll need to use map and compass to navigate through the timber to reach an open slope that you can take to the summit. The route gets steep but is non-technical.

The main trail continues north through the spruce forest and small clearings. Past the last meadow, the trail turns toward the east and descends along the nose of a ridge, avoiding the much steeper slope just around the corner to the west. You connect with Trail 1848 just after leaving the wilderness boundary.

SOUTH DERBY TRAIL 1857

Description

This trail offers a short walk onto the plateau, *but only if your vehicle can handle the road.* The path climbs fast and for a short distance it ascends a very steep wall, using switchbacks.

Destination

Island Lakes, Trail 1842

Distance

3 miles

Elevation

10,760, 11,180

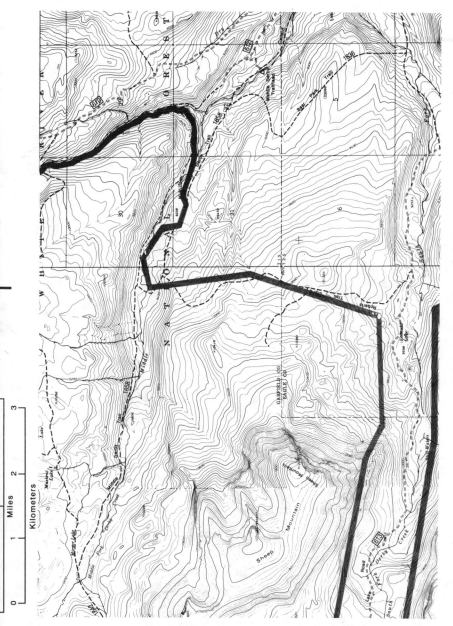

Roberts Trail 2076. Map 122 East
— Trails Illustrated Topo Map.

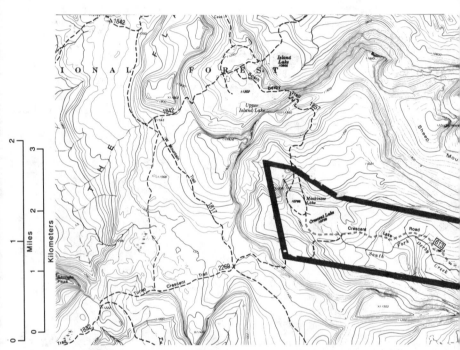

Turret Crescent Trail 2269, and W Mountain Trail, 1817 South Derby Trail 1857, Map 122, East — **Trails Illustrated Topo Map.**

Directions to trailhead

From Eagle County Road 39, go west on Forest Road 613, twelve miles to Crescent Lake and the trailhead.

Maps

Trappers Lake

The W Mountain Trail heading north from the Island Lake Trail.

Getting there is half the fun. The road to the trailhead is challenging. The trail begins between Crescent and Mackinaw Lakes at the bottom of a glacially carved gorge. Northeast of the lakes are several unnamed pothole lakes, scattered across the hummocky terrain, left behind when the sheet of ice melted.

After walking along the east shore of Mackinaw, (the west lake), you begin a gradual climb that becomes radically steeper as you ascend the wall of the gorge. Switchbacks make the short ascent somewhat easier. Once on top, you will see Upper Island Lake and several small potholes on the flat west of Upper Island. Look back to the east to see scattered ponds on the timbered flat northeast of Mackinaw Lake. From there, it's less than one-half mile to Trail 1842. You can also see Island Lake, three hundred feet below your boots to the north. Trail 1842 is the easiest route to Island Lake, which has suitable campsites in the timber along the north shore. The Island Lakes have cutthroats.

TURRET—CRESCENT TRAIL 2269

Description

This climb is much less severe than Trail 1857. Once on top, you'll cross the nearly level plateau in the shadow of Shingle Peak.

Destination

Trail 1817, Trail 1832 and Shingle Peak

Distance

2, 4 miles

Elevation

10,760, 11,490

Directions to trailhead

From Eagle County Road 39, go west on Forest Road 613, twelve miles to Crescent Lake and the trailhead.

Maps

Trappers Lake (See Page 166)

This is another trail accessed from the Crescent Lake trailhead. It gets you onto the Flat Tops a little quicker than the other route, Trail 1857. It's about 1.5 miles from the lakes to the top.

Once up on the flat, you see dozens of potholes east of Shingle Peak. The 1.5 mile walk past the lakes is high meadow, with only scattered stands of timber on the plateau. Straight west is Shingle Peak, a massive basaltic mountain having horizontal and vertical fractures giving it the appearance of a shingled roof when the light is just right. Sunrise or sunset, when the light plays off the peak, accentuating the dull red tones of the eroding basalt, are the two best times to view the mountain.

Just east of the peak on the flat, the trail connects with Trail 1832 and a spur that leads north below the peak. Going left on 1832 will take you down Turret Creek to Sweetwater Lake. Continuing west, you connect with Trail 2042 after a 1.5 mile walk. From 2042, it's another mile to Trail 1816.

FOREST ROAD 616

This road goes south from Forest Road 613 four miles past the Derby Loop Road. It has the same problems as the other road as it travels across volcanic rubble and clay soils. It's not quite two miles to the end of the road and the W Mountain Trailhead.

W MOUNTAIN TRAIL 1817

Description

W Mountain is the one with the distinctive east face you see from State Highway 131. As its name suggests, it appears as the letter W. The feature is more easily noticed in the early spring, when there's still snow on the plateau.

Most of the climb on this trail occurs in the first three miles. Once up on the plateau, hiking is much easier. Carry plenty of water, though, or else plan on long detours to refill your canteens.

Destination

W Mountain and Trail 2060, Trail 2269, Trail 1842

Distance

5, 8, 10 miles

Elevation

9,570, 11,739

Directions to trailhead

From Eagle County Road 39, go west on Forest Road 613, five miles to the junction of Forest Road 616. Go left, to the south. Two miles to the trailhead. The road takes you through an area burned in the summer of 1979. As with other roads in the area, you must contend with volcanic rubble and soils to reach this trailhead.

Maps

Sugarloaf Mountain, Sweetwater Lake, Trappers Lake (See Pages 166, 171)

The W Mountain Trail heading north from the Island Lake Trail.

It is advisable to carry plenty of water on this trail, because there are several stretches on which none is available. The trail begins at the end of Forest Road 616 at a place called Big Spring. It heads west up a moderate slope before turning to traverse the grade. From there it generally follows a small canyon above an unnamed creek. The trail continues climbing, but the ascent is gradual except in a couple of places near the head of the canyon.

W Mountain is not really a definable peak but more of a high point along the rim. When you reach the top of the plateau, look to the north where you will see a 200-foot rampart. Buck and Star lakes are just below this point. They're about one-half mile off the trail. There is no path leading to the lakes.

On top, the trail meanders through a high open meadow, climbing gradually to cross W Mountain. From here, you cross to the west side of the high ridge to overlook a glacially scoured drainage 1,300 feet below. The trail heads north along a narrowing ridge past the 11,850-foot summit of the very broad W Mountain. The high point of the trail is one-half mile farther north at 11,739 feet, where the ridge is only a couple hundred yards across. Look east here to view Bull Lake, nearly 800 feet below.

Another mile along the trail brings you to Trail 2269. To the west of this intersection, you'll get a look at Shingle Peak. North of the trail junction, you pass the head of the South Fork of Derby

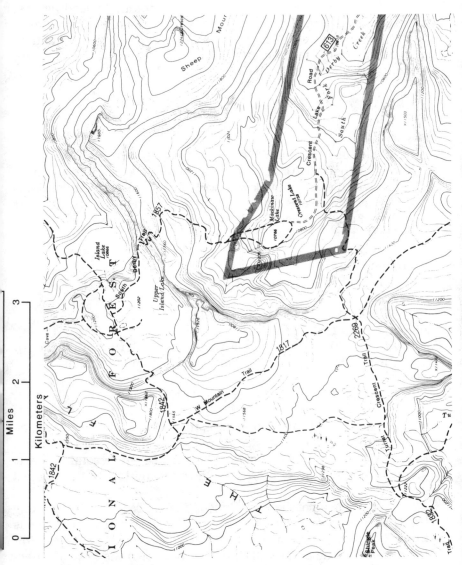

W. Mountain Trail 1817, Part 1 and Crescent Lake
Trail 2269 (See also, Derby Trail 1857)
— **Trails Illustrated Topo Map.**

Creek. Near the head of this glacial valley can be seen Crescent and Mackinaw lakes.

The junction of Trail 1842, which leads east past the two Island Lakes, is two miles north of trail 2269. From here, the trail wanders along the basaltic plateau below a long, low, north-trending hill to the east. Another mile takes you to a crossover to Trail 1816

From this junction, the trail climbs gradually, leading past a couple of unnamed pothole lakes and through a willow grove. Past the willows, the trail heads northeast over a nearly flat plateau before beginning an almost imperceptible descent to Trail 1120, which takes you to Stillwater Reservoir and Forest Road 900.

SOUTH W MOUNTAIN TRAIL 2060

Description

A mile southwest of W Mountain, this trail heads south to connect with Trail 2032. It departs from the W Mountain Trail at the south end of a willow grove. As on Trail 1817, the hike is across the treeless plateau until you reach the head of the West Fork of Sheep Creek

Destination

Trail 2032

Distance

3 1/2 miles

Elevation

11,500 at Trail 1817, 10,110 at Trail 2032

Directions to trail

From Trail 1817, four miles west of Big Spring Trailhead, or three miles south of the Trails 1817—2269 junction.

Maps

Sugarloaf Mountain, Sweetwater Lake

The first mile of your walk is through a grove of willows, as the trail follows the west side of the uniquely-shaped mountain. Below to the west, the sides of the plateau steepen, becoming nearly vertical, dropping away more than a thousand feet to the wooded slopes below.

At the head of the West Fork of Sheep Creek, two miles along the trail, the route begins a descent. The head of the drainage is broad but as you hike downward, the sides close in. The path follows the west side of the valley, taking you down the nose of a narrow, timber-covered ridge for a ways, using switchbacks to keep the grade moderate. At the bottom of the descent, the slope flattens.

Here, you connect with Trail 2032. Carry plenty of water, as the only sources along this trail are intermittent headwater streams.

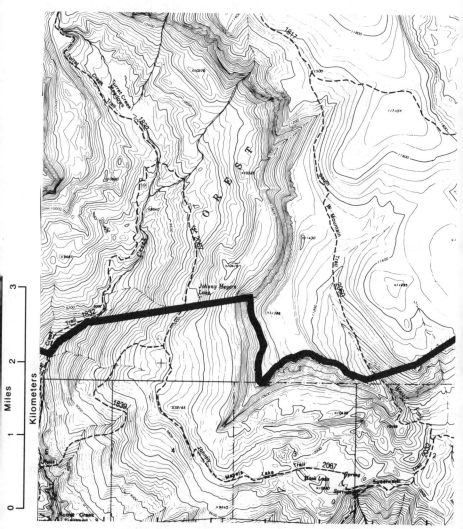

South W Mountain Trail 2060. And Johnny Meyers Lake Trail 2067 — **Trails Illustrated Topo Map.**

EAGLE COUNTY ROAD 40

From State Highway 131, twenty-eight miles south on Eagle County Road 301 to Eagle County Road 40. Go west, to the right. It's seven miles along this gravel road to the Garfield County line, where the designation changes to Garfield County Road 150. From there, it's three miles to Sweetwater Lake, then two more miles to the end of the road.

TURRET CREEK TRAIL 1832

Description

This trail follows Turret Creek. You're going uphill all the way to Shingle Peak, seven miles away. For the climb, you stay close to the creek so water won't be a problem.

Destination

Trail 1839, Trail 2067, Turret Peak, Shingle Peak, Trail 2269

Distance

1/2, 5, 7, 8 miles

Elevation

8,000, 11,222

Directions to trailhead

West on Eagle County Road 40, twelve miles to end of the road past Sweetwater Lake. Unless you have four-wheel-drive, park at bottom of the steep grade in the small marked area by the road. From there, it's one-half mile to the trailhead.

Maps

Sweetwater Lake, Trappers Lake

Turret Peak seen from near Shingle Peak. Turret Peak is between the Turret Creek and Shingle Peak trails.

The first mile of Trail 1832 is through private property so stay on the trail. After going around the end of a ridge, you skirt the edge of the timber as you ascend the narrow canyon drained by Turret Creek. In the first two miles, you climb a thousand feet. The next two miles takes you up another 600 feet, where you emerge from the trees into Turret Creek Meadows, a one-half mile-long opening.

The trail passes the meadow along the west side, where you begin another ascent in the shadow of 11,525-foot Turret Peak. The peak isn't large. It's a cone-shaped mountain, timbered all the way to the top. The east face, though, is a sharp dropoff, falling away more than 600 feet. Over the next mile, you pass in and out of the timber in sight of the tiny creek. When you break into the open for the last short ascent, you have a view of a falls dropping nearly forty feet.

The gradient is gentle as you approach Shingle Peak from the south. Hiking 1.5 miles past the falls, you connect with Trail 2269 below the peak. Over the next two miles, the trail wanders through the high tundra below the basaltic mountain. After a mile, you reach the northern terminus of Trail 2042. Continuing on, you connect with Trail 1816.

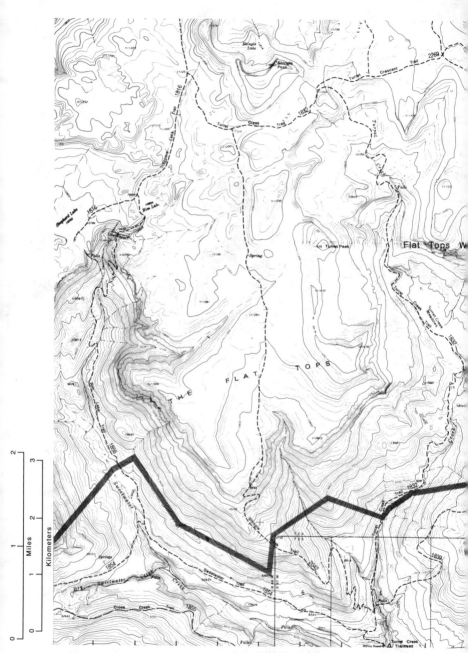

Turret Creek Trail 1832, Shingle Peak Trail, 2042, and Rim Lake Trail 1856, Map 122 East —**Trails Illustrated Topo Map.**

SHINGLE PEAK TRAIL 2042

Description

This is a trail that will test your heart, lungs, and legs. It climbs 2,600 feet in the first four miles. Once you reach the plateau, the hike is nearly flat over the next three miles to Trail 1832. Water is scarce on this trail.

Destination

Trail 1832

Distance

7 miles

Elevation

8,000, 11,115

Directions to trail

From the Turret Creek Trailhead above Sweetwater Lake, west one-half mile on Trail 1854 to junction of Trail 1832. Follow this path around the ridge to a three-way junction near the falls on Turret Creek. Trail 2042 heads west up the steep slope.

Maps

Sweetwater Lake, Trappers Lake (See Page 176)

Trail 2042 is the second junction along Trail 1832, one-half

Shingle Peak seen from Rim Lake on the Trappers Lake Trail.

mile past the Turret Creek Trailhead. It begins on an open slope, climbing the nose of the ridge, using switchbacks to get you up the slope. After passing the first opening in the timber, you reach a junction in the trail. To the right is a trail connecting to Trail 1832 and Turret Creek. Go left to stay on Trail 2042.

At the second opening on the ridge, the trail swings left, returning to the nose of the ridge to continue upward. You reach the plateau two miles farther north. At that point, you have ascended 2,600 feet in only four miles.

On the flat, you still climb but the gradient is much lower, nearly unnoticeable. After 2.5 miles of meandering through timber and open parks, you reach a fork in the trail. The left fork takes you to Rim Lake and Trails 1856 and 1816. Trail 2042 goes to the right here. Near the fork is a pond and a spring. This is the first water source since leaving the trailhead five miles back. You come to Trail 1832 at the base of Shingle Peak 1.5 miles past the fork.

JOHNNY MEYERS LAKE TRAIL 2067

Description

This trail takes you to Johnny Meyers Lake, at the Wilderness boundary. The route leads through the wooded slope seen from the plateau near W Mountain. while the ground is rough and uneven, the elevation varies little.

Destination

Trail 1839, Trail 2032

Distance

1 1/2, 5 miles

Elevation

9,600 at Trail 1832, 10,060 1 mile west of Hack Lake, 9,800 at Trail 2032

Directions to trail

From trail 1832, 3.5 miles from the Turret Creek Trailhead, or four miles from the junction of Trail 2269.

The trail is also accessed from Trail 2032, three miles from the Sweetwater Guard Station.

Maps

Sweetwater Lake (See Page 173)

The trail crosses Turret Creek one-half mile south of Turret Creek Meadows. It generally follows a ledge above a steeper slope through the timber on the way to Johnny Meyers Lake, a pothole left behind by the glaciers. The small flats north and south of the lake offer camp sites.

A few yards past the lake, the trail exits the Wilderness. It wanders south, then east across the timbered slope. West of Hack Lake, meadows appear and the broad ledge becomes less challenging. From the east side of the lake, the trail descends across a steep slope to join Trail 2032. Several springs in this area are a source of water.

SWEETWATER TRAIL 1854

Description

This trail generally follows Sweetwater and Dry Sweetwater creeks, between the Turret Creek and Indian Camp trailheads. The route gives access to three trails that take you into the Wilderness.

Destination

Trail 1856, Indian Camp Pass

Distance

3, 7 miles

Elevation

8,000, 9,724

Directions to trailhead

From State Highway 131, twenty-eight miles south on Eagle County Road 301 to Eagle County Road 40. West twelve miles to trailhead past Sweetwater Lake. Unless you have four-wheel-drive, park at bottom of the steep grade in a marked area by the road. From there, it's one-half mile to the trail head.

Maps

Deep Lake, Sweetwater Lake, Trappers Lake

The Turret Creek Trailhead, 2 miles west of Sweetwater Lake. This trailhead gives access to the 1839, Turret Creek, Shingle Peak, and Sweetwater trails.

This trail doesn't go into the Wilderness, but it gives access to Trail 1856, which does. The junction is the first left, past the trailhead. It follows the upper slope of the canyon drained by Sweetwater Creek, which you see more than 200 feet below.

Trail 1856, which takes you to Rim Lake, is three miles up the trail. You also cross the main fork of Sweetwater Creek here. From the crossing, the path turns abruptly south to follow around the end of the ridge and wander up along Dry Sweetwater Creek. You cross the small stream just east of Triangle Mountain that rises abruptly a mile ahead. You reach Indian Camp Pass and Forest Road 600 two miles farther west, after walking past large beaver ponds.

RIM LAKE TRAIL 1856

Description

As is typical of the trails on the southeast side of the plateau, this one climbs rapidly. It follows Sweetwater Creek to its source, so water isn't a problem. The path stays at the bottom of the draw until you near the headwall of the canyon, where it climbs out rather sharply.

Destination

Rim Lake, Trail 1816

Distance

5 miles

Elevation

8,530 at Trail 1854, 10,826 at Trail 1816

Directions to trail

From the Turret Creek Trailhead, three miles west on Trail 1854 or four miles east from Indian Camp Pass.

Maps

Sweetwater Lake, Trappers Lake (See Page 176)

Shingle Peak and Rim Lake on the Rim Lake Trail.

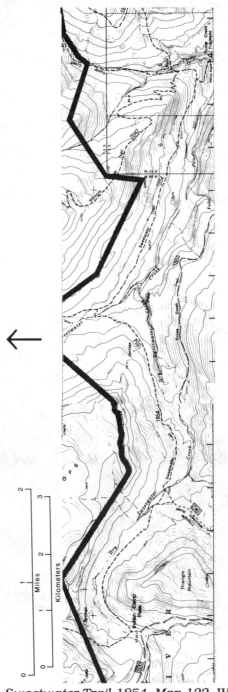

Sweetwater Trail 1854. Map 122, West &
122 East — **Trails Illustrated Topo Map.**

The upper Sweetwater Creek drainage descends a steep, rugged, glacially scoured canyon. From Trail 1854, the bottom of the canyon is nearly flat and broad. A mile north and just across the Wilderness boundary, the stream drains a large boggy area. The trail keeps to the higher ground east of the swamp, where it begins climbing across a steep, rocky, open slope. Here, the ascent becomes steeper, leading onto a small ledge where you can take a breather.

The trail crosses the creek a short distance farther, then begins another steady climb. You cross a second open slope, then skirt a grove of low brush before crossing Sweetwater Creek again. From this point, the climb becomes serious. You work your way up and around a steep slope covered with slide rock. If you look up the fork of the creek coming from the northwest, you'll see a series of falls as the stream tumbles down the nearly vertical wall. Take a break and dig out your camera before continuing on. Also, remember that you have less than a mile to go to reach the plateau.

Near the top of the canyon, the trail makes a turn to the east and follows a more gentle slope along Sweetwater Creek. You break out into the open almost in sight of Rim Lake, aptly named for its position on the edge of the plateau. Past the lake, 0.1 mile north, you connect with Trail 1816. Here, you can go left and descend to Indian Camp Pass, or go north to Trappers Lake.

Forest Road 600

Eagle County Road 17, at Deep Creek, leaves Eagle County Road 301 thirty-four miles south from State Highway 131, and 1.5 miles north from Interstate 70. After crossing the National Forest boundary, the road designation changes to Forest Road 600. Fourteen miles from County Road 301 is a spur to the right leading to the Deep Creek Overlook. At eighteen miles, you come to Broken Rib Spring, a good source of water. Forest Road 601, leading west to Heart Lake, is twenty-nine miles from Eagle County Road 301. Another mile takes you to Deep Lake. The road this far is narrow but in good condition because of logging. Watch out for the log trucks as the drivers are unlikely to yield to others.

From Deep Lake, it's five miles to Indian Camp Pass, then three more miles to The Meadows, and another mile to Budge's White River Resort and the end of the road, a distance of thirty-nine miles. Allow about two hours to drive the entire distance. Drivers of vehicles with low clearance should not drive much past Deep Lake. All other roads in the environmentally challenged area are very rough.

Deep Creek Canyon

DEEP CREEK OVERLOOK

You hear the roar of Deep Creek, subdued by the 2,300-foot drop below the limestone rim. From the overlook on the south rim, you can look across to the other side and see caves in the limestone wall. The deep gorge is another feature found on the Flat Tops created by the sheet of ice that covered the region a few thousand years ago.

Most visitors will be satisfied to simply stop and look upon this magnificent vista, a sight unequaled elsewhere in the Wilderness. For the adventurous, game trails lead down the vertical sides into the depths of the gorge.

The overlook is on Forest Road 600, fourteen miles from Eagle County Road 301. The spur road is marked with a sign. Park and walk over to the rim. A chain link fence protects you from the severe exposure. Camping is not permitted in the immediate area.

Current information on the following trails is available from:
Eagle Ranger District
White River National Forest
125 W. 5th St.
PO Box 720
Eagle, CO 81631
(303) 328-6388

TRAPPERS LAKE TRAIL 1816

Description
> This one traverses the Wilderness from south to north, eventually taking you to Trappers Lake. You climb a thousand feet in the first 1.5 miles but once on top, the walk is easy. You can also make this hike from Trappers Lake.

Destination
> Indian Lake, Shepherd Lake, Trail 1856, Rim Lake, Trail 2269, Trail 1818, Trail 1803, Trail 1815

Distance
> 4, 6, 7, 9, 12, 13, 17 miles

Elevation
> 9,724, 11,275

Directions to trailhead
> Thirty-five miles from Eagle County Road 301 on Forest Road 600 to Indian Camp Pass and trailhead. Sign at the trailhead may be confusing. Arrows indicate Trail 1816 is to the west and Trail 1854 is straight ahead. 1816 ascends the slope directly to the north and 1854 follows the canyon, toward the east. You can see Trail 1816 quite plainly on the slope.

Maps
> Deep Lake, Sweetwater Lake, Trappers Lake (See Pages 103, 104)

Easy hiking near Indian Lake on the Trappers Lake Trail.

The climb is steady as you ascend the slope to the plateau. It cuts across the rise, though, so it isn't too bad a climb. You top out on the plateau where the grade is much more gentle as you head northeast. At two miles, the way is nearly level and you make good time across the wooded flat. Interspersed with the trees are broad open expanses of green meadows.

You pass a few pothole lakes on the way to Indian Lake, four miles from the start of your walk, right of the trail. Another two miles takes you to Shepherd Lake on the west side of the trail. It lies in a broad opening. The timber on the south side well away from the lake, is suitable for camping.

Just past the crossing of the outlet stream from Shepherd, you connect with a path going east that leads to Trail 1856, which comes in from the south up a fork of Sweetwater Creek. Either route, Trail 1816 to the left or 1856 to the right will get you to Rim Lake, one mile farther north.

Rim Lake sits at the head of the canyon drained by Sweetwater Creek and is the stream's source. It's out in the open. The tallest vegetation around it is the willows that crowd the shoreline in places.

From either lake, your view of 11,996-foot Shingle Peak to the northeast is unobstructed. The peak is one of the remnants of the volcanism that covered the Flat Tops over the past seventy million years. It rises only about 800 feet above the plateau, but is impressive due to its massive size. This basaltic mountain is appropriately named as the fracture pattern in the rock and its color at sunset causes it to appear as the roof of a giant's barn, covered with red shingles. You'll get the best photos of the peak at sunset from the west side.

As you travel north, your walk leads past several small pothole lakes scattered about the plateau. Two miles from Rim Lake, you'll connect with trail 1832 due west of Shingle Peak. This trail will take you east to the Shingle Peak, Turret Creek, and W Mountain Trails.

For the next two miles, your hike is through high meadows below and west of the peak. Two miles from the junction with Trail 1832 you cross the outlet of Shingle Lake. The lake sits on a shelf below the north slope of Shingle Peak, a mile south of the trail. No path leads to it, but by following the stream, you'll find it alright.

The stream exiting Shingle Lake is one of several that form the headwaters of the South Fork of the White River. At the creek, you can look below and see the river flowing southwest at the bottom of an 800-foot gorge.

A mile north of the Shingle Lake outlet stream, you cross the main branch of the South Fork's headwaters. The water collects in a cluster of potholes scattered about the plateau to the north. Continuing north another one-quarter mile, you connect with Trail 1818, which leads to Wall Lake and Trappers Peak to the west.

The flat to the north and west of the trail junction is covered with pothole lakes, the headwaters of the South Fork of the White River. One note of interest here is that both forks of the White River head in this area within a mile of each other.

About one mile past Trail 1818, you come to the junction of Trail 1842, which leads east to Island Lake and the W Mountain trail. Here, Trail 1816 begins a rapid descent on the way down the glacial valley leading to Trappers Lake. Near the head of the valley one mile down the trail from the plateau, you pass within a short distance of Parvin Lake, located in a cirque below the west wall. You should be able to find camp sites on the flats north and south of the lake.

Past Parvin, the descent becomes more gradual, almost flat in places in the next three miles, where you connect with Trail 1815, the one that takes you around the shoreline of Trappers Lake. Going left at the junction will take you to the Scotts Bay Trailhead, a distance of two miles if you follow the lake shore. Taking the right fork leads to Trail 1814. Follow it north past the Division of Wildlife cabins to the Outlet Trailhead.

SWEETWATER TRAIL 1854

Description
This trail follows the Dry Sweetwater Creek drainage as it takes you east. It doesn't enter the Wilderness, but connects with trails that take you there. The trail ends at the other trailhead above Sweetwater Lake, so can be hiked from either direction.
Destination
Trail 1856, Sweetwater Lake area
Distance
5, 9 miles
Elevation
9,724, 8,000
Directions to trailhead
Thirty-five miles from Eagle County Road 301 on Forest Road 600 to Indian Camp Pass and trailhead. Sign at the trailhead may be confusing. Arrows indicate Trail 1816 is to the west and Trail 1854 is straight ahead. 1816 ascends the slope directly to the north and 1854 follows the canyon, toward the east.

Maps
Deep Lake, Sweetwater Lake (See Page 182)
For trail description, see listing under Eagle County Road 40

FAWN CREEK TRAIL 1838

Description
This is an alternate route to Shepherd and Rim Lakes. For the backpacker, it won't save time or miles. Used mainly for horse travel.

Destination
Elk Knob, Trail 1816

Distance
4, 6 miles

Elevation
9,095, 10,600

Directions to trailhead
West on Eagle County Road 17 at Deep Creek, which becomes Forest Road 600 at the National Forest boundary. Thirty-eight miles from County Road 301 to The Meadows and trailhead.

Maps
Deep Lake

The path is easy to see once you've found it. The trail begins to the right of the sign by the road. There is no information there concerning the trail. Look directly east and you'll notice the barely discernable path. A few feet farther, it crosses Fawn Creek, the stream directly north of the parking area. The best way to find the trail is cross the creek, then follow it up the slope. There, the trail is more distinct.

It climbs the steep slope as it follows Fawn Creek to its source on the plateau. You walk in the open most of the way until you reach the top. From there, you can head east, going cross-country to connect with Trail 1816, which will take you to Shepherd and Rim lakes. Budge's uses this route to these lakes, so you can follow the horse path to the trail.

Current information on the following trails is available from:

Blanco Ranger District
White River National Forest
317 E. Market
PO Box 7
Meeker, CO 81649
(303) 878-4039

*The Meadows Trail 1827, Fawn Creek Trail
1838, and Trail 2259. Map122, West
— **Trails Illustrated Topo Map.***

189

SOUTH FORK TRAIL 1827—THE MEADOWS

Description

    This part of the trail takes you on an easy walk along the beautiful upper South Fork of the White River. It leads north along the broad stream plain. Except for the willows growing along the stream, there's nothing to interfere with your view of the valley of the South Fork.

Destination

    Trail 1830 and Trail 2259

Distance

    2 miles

Elevation

    9,000 at The Meadows, 9,170 at trail junction

Directions to trailhead

    West on Eagle County Road 17 at Deep Creek, which becomes Forest Road 600 at the National Forest boundary. Thirty-eight miles from County Road 301 to The Meadows and trailhead.

Maps

    Big Marvine Peak, Deep Lake, Trappers Lake (See Page 189)

The Meadows Trailhead gives access to the upper South Fork of the White River, Fawn Creek, Nichols Creek, and Doe Creek trails.

This section of the trail is an easy hike through the broad valley. It's used primarily by anglers to access the river. Past the junction of the Trail 2259 at Doe Creek, a path continues upstream along the river. It's not maintained, but gets enough traffic to keep it visible and easy to follow. If your main interest here is fishing, backpack in a few miles, where you'll find camping near the stream.

Access to the river along the first mile, near The Meadows, is a challenge. From the trail, the willows growing along the White don't look bad. They're almost impenetrable, though. Deer like to hide in the thickets. The dense cover provides concealment and browse for them close to water.

Above the river, the canyon walls rise gently at first, then nearly vertically. The lower slopes are open, covered with high grasses and low brush here and there. The ground is hummocky in places along the river, the result of unstable conditions created when the glaciers left behind piles of rubble in the valley. You'll also find ponds scattered along the river. Approach them quietly and you may catch a glance at a mama Teal and her babies, hatched in the early summer.

Water is abundant along this trail. There are springs along the west bank a couple of miles upstream from the Doe Creek trail junction. On the east bank, several tiny streams come rushing down the steep sides to join the White.

NICHOLS CREEK TRAIL 1830

Description

It's two miles of climbing followed by three miles of pleasant hiking. The trail gets a lot of horse traffic from Budge's Resort.

Destination

Trail 1829, Trail 1828, Trail 1825

Distance

2, 4, 5 miles

Elevation

9,170 at the South Fork, 11,018 at Trail 1825

Directions to trail

Two miles north from The Meadows along Trail 1827. At the junction, this trail begins at Nichols Creek and heads west up the steep slope. The sign at the trailhead spells the name Nichole Creek.

Maps

Big Marvine Peak, Deep Lake (See Page 60)

191

Lost Solar Park camp near the junction of the
Nichols Creek and Park Creek trails.

You have to make a stream crossing to reach this trail. The difficult part will be keeping your feet dry. The White isn't large here, but it's still too wide to jump across and there are no logs to scramble over to the other side. Unless you have waders along, it's probably best to remove your boots and wade across.

Nichols Creek is a small trickle of water that plunges in a nearly straight line down the canyon wall. The trail follows close by on the north side of the stream. There are few meanders on the route, but the hike isn't as bad as it seems. The hillside is open, covered in grass and low brush. There are a couple of bogs to cross. One has timbers placed in the muck so you won't sink in too deep. You pass beside light timber on the way up in a few places. Near the head of the small drainage, the slope begins to ease. It gives the feeling of seeing the light at the end of the tunnel. You're almost there.

At the rim, the walk is suddenly easy, having a nearly imperceptible gradient. A small pond awaits on top, an inviting place to sit and recover from your exertion. Here, you connect with Trail 1829, which leads down Park Creek. The plateau area south of the trail has a large number of pothole lakes. If you're interested in fishing, check with the Division of Wildlife to learn if any have been stocked and the expected conditions.

The trail now wanders westward through large, grassy parks. It climbs slightly, but the hike now is easy. As the route veers north, you come in view of Timber Mountain on the right, east of the trail. It rises to 11,425 feet, but doesn't appear impressive since it's only 600 feet to the top. Directly west of the peak and left of the trail lies Horseshoe Lake. Get to it from the small clearing. You'll have a short hike from it through the timber to the lake.

Past Timber Mountain, the trail continues north, leading to Trail 1828, Lost Solar Creek, and Lost Solar Park. One mile further, you reach Trail 1830, which continues on to Trail 1825.

Finding a camp site along this trail won't be a problem.

Once you're on the plateau, you'll be in elk country. The dense timber gives good cover, where they go to rest and chew their cuds after feeding in the many grassy parks.

TRAIL 2259

Description

This hike takes you to the barren open country in the heart of the Flat Tops Plateau. On top, Trail 1825 connects with Trail 1823, which leads down Marvine Creek.

Destination

Trail 1825

Distance

5 miles

Elevation

9,095, 11,050 near Doe creek, 10,954 at Trail 1825

Directions to trail

Two miles north from the Meadows along Trail 1827. At the junction, this trail begins beside Doe Creek and ascends a grassy slope to the north.

Maps

Deep Lake (See Page 189)

Doe Creek Falls, north of the South Fork of the White River.

As on the Nichols Creek Trail, you must cross the river to reach this one, too. On the west bank, the trail continues upstream along the South Fork to Doe Creek. Here, the trail leaves the river and begins a gentle climb up and across a grassy slope.

About a mile from the river, you pass a small patch of timber, then continue on across the steepening hillside. Along the way, you pass a few springs below the trail. The next mile is a bit steeper as the path zigzags up the slope toward the head of a small, unnamed drainage. A little farther and you break out on top of the plateau.

The next three miles are easy — a casual stroll leading past a surface pockmarked with potholes. In that distance, the trail rises about 200 feet, then falls about 50 or so feet as you descend to cross the headwaters of Doe Creek.

At the confluence of Doe Creek and the South Fork, an old, no longer maintained trail follows Doe Creek upstream. Doe Creek Falls, a senic place worth the detour, is located two miles from the South Fork up this path. The fall isn't high, only about 50 or 60 feet. The scene is worth the walk, though. The water plunges over a cleft in the black basalt. The grassy hillside downstream from the falls is a good place to see elk.

SOUTH FORK TRAIL 1827

Description

The trail follows the South Fork of the White River to the South Fork Campground. This is a reverse route of the same trail described on page 53.

Destination

Trail 1829, Trail 1828, South Fork CG

Distance

5, 8, 13 miles

Elevation

9,095, 7,602

Directions to trailhead

West on Eagle County Road 17 at Deep Creek, which becomes Forest Road 600 at the National Forest boundary. Go west past The Meadows to a rail fence and gate, the entrance to Budge's White River Resort. Be sure to close the gate. From the gate, it's just a short distance to the parking area on the right. Thirty-nine miles from County Road 301 to the trail head.

Maps

Big Marvine Creek, Deep Lake, Lost Park, Oyster Lake (See Pages 58-60)

See South Fork Campground Trailhead for description of the trail.

Current information on the following trails is available from:

Rifle Ranger District
White River National Forest
0094 County Road 94
Rifle, CO 81650
(303) 625-2371

WAGONWHEEL CREEK TRAIL 2049

Description

An easy walk through a beautiful stream plain. The last 1.5 miles takes you down the nose of a ridge to Budge's White River Resort. You can hike it from either end. This trail is a good one to ride if you're staying at Budge's. With horses, you could make a long trip by following this one south, then go over to Patterson Creek Trail. Could be a good one or two night trail ride.

Destination

South Fork of the White River and Budge's White River Resort

Distance

6 miles

Elevation

10,770, 10,480

Directions to trailhead

West on Eagle County Road 17 at Deep Creek, which becomes Forest Road 600 at the National Forest boundary. Twenty-nine miles to Forest Road 601. Sign, Heart Lake 1 mile. At 0.6 miles, bear left by Klines Folly CG to Bison Lake. At Supply Basin CG, another 0.9 miles, to junction. Go right on Forest Road 640 past Heart Lake on the north. Continue past Bison Lake to junction of Forest Road 645, 3.4 miles from Forest Road 600. Go right on Forest Road 645, 1.6 miles to junction with Forest Road 644, the Dry Buck Loop. Go left at junction 0.6 miles to unmarked trail head above Wagonwheel Creek. High-clearance four-wheel-drive required on Forest Road 645 and Forest Road 644.

Maps

Blair Mountain, Deep Lake

Wagonwheel Creek Trailhead.

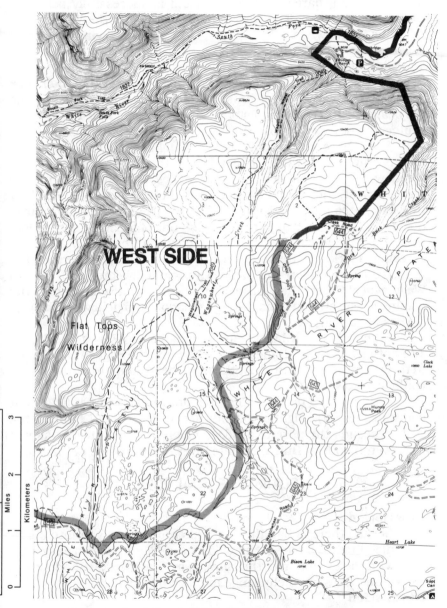

Wagonwheel Creek Trail 2049. Map 122, West & 123 West — **Trails Illustrated Topo Map.**

The only indication of the trailhead is a sign giving scant Wilderness information at the end of the road. The path is a former two-track road, barely visible because it is successfully being reclaimed by the land. The trail wanders north into the Wilderness, following Wagonwheel Creek, a tiny, clear stream flowing over a bed of limestone cobbles. It takes the hunter into good areas for deer and elk that don't require horses to access.

The remnants of beaver ponds can be seen one-half mile north along the creek, now broken and no longer maintained since the beavers left. From a limestone rim one-quarter mile north of the trailhead, your view across the large meadow is unhindered.

You have several options for hiking in this area. About one mile northwest from the trailhead, past the marshy, beaver pond meadow, the trail splits into three branches. The left fork continues on northwest, then bends around toward the south. You can follow this fork three miles to Forest Road 640. The first half of the trail takes you through open parks along stands of pine and spruce forests. The hike is nearly level. The second half begins at a stream crossing, a fork of Patterson Creek to the west. When you reach the road, you can return the same way, or follow the road east to Wagonwheel Creek, then follow it cross-country downstream to the trailhead. The stream runs through meadowland, following the Wilderness boundary.

The right fork heads east, taking you to Forest Road 644. The path leads through meadows and along the edge of woodlands in the 1.5 miles to the road. At the road, head south to return to the trailhead.

By heading north at the junction, you stay on Trail 2049. It continues north in sight of Wagonwheel Creek. After 1.5 miles, the path descends the nose of a ridge, which becomes steeper as you get lower. It ends at Budge's White River Resort beside Cabin No. 1.

BLAIR LAKE TRAIL 2098

Description

Getting there is half the fun. This route takes you into a scenic, little used part of the Wilderness. The trail is an easy walk with the exception of the climb near Crater Lake. Shadow and Blair Lakes are a challenge to reach off the trail.

Destination

Jet Lake, Shadow Lake, Blair Lake, Crater Lake, Crater Lake Trailhead

Distance

2, 3, 3.5, 5, 6 miles

Elevation

10,390, 11,100 (Descends to 9,960 east of Crater Lake)

Directions to trailhead

The southwest area of the Flat Tops is a place having some of the most challenging roads you'll ever drive. Few are steep, but they are exceedingly rough, requiring high-clearance four-wheel-drive vehicles to bounce over boulders and work your way through bogs. The roads are rough enough that you can often walk just as quickly as drive. A four-wheel-drive will save you a few miles of carrying a pack, though. Carry a high-lift jack or a winch and travel with two vehicles when possible. This may not be essential, but it will ease the job of extracting a stuck or high-centered vehicle.

Patterson Creek Trailhead

West on Eagle County Road 17 at Deep Creek, which becomes Forest Road 600 at the National Forest boundary. Twenty-nine miles to Forest Road 601. Sign, Heart Lake 1 mile. At 0.6 miles, bear left by Klines Folly CG to Bison Lake. At Supply Basin CG, another 0.9 miles, to junction. Go right on Forest Road 640 past Heart Lake on the north. Continue past Bison Lake to junction of Forest Road 645, 3.4 miles from Forest Road 600. Go left, staying on Forest Road 640. It's five miles to Elk Lakes trailhead over a very rough road. Sign at trailhead.

Crater Lake Trailhead

South from Buford on Rio Blanco County Road 17 toward New Castle. Inside the National Forest, the designation changes to Forest Road 245. Eleven miles from Buford, turn east at Hiner Spring on Forest Road 601. Three miles farther, you will need four-wheel-drive. Another 0.5 miles to a junction. Go left. A second junction in another 0.5 miles. The left fork travels the flat above the rim overlooking the South Fork of the White River and ends at the trailhead. You'll pass through two gates going this way.

The right fork is Forest Road 601. It takes you south two miles to a junction. Go left. 0.5 miles further is a junction by Cow Lake. Go left, leaving Forest Road 601. From there, it's a little more than two miles to the trailhead.

Maps

Blair Mountain

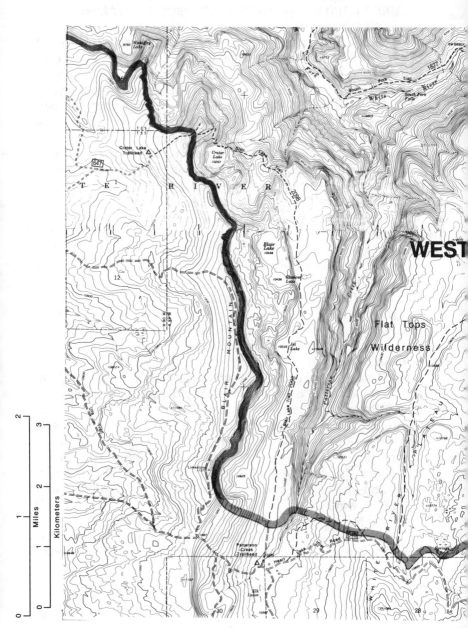

Blair Lake Trail 2098. Map 122, West, 123,
West — **Trails Illustrated Topo Map.**

The Crater Lake Trail goes north at the
base of the cliffs of Blair Mountain.

Once you've arrived at the trailhead, the hike is easy. At Patterson Creek, head north along an old road leading to the Wilderness boundary one-half mile away. The first mile is through an open flat. To the west, you see the vertical limestone cliff-face of Blair Mountain, which you follow for the length of the trail. Above the timbered slope to the west and below the cliff, is an unnamed lake. No trail leads to the lake and expect downed timber along the way.

As you continue north, the route takes you through timber and scattered openings. After two miles, you pass along the east shore of Jet Lake. A mile north of Jet Lake, the trail passes below a short but steep timbered cliff. Above it lie Shadow and Blair Lakes. Reaching them requires bushwhacking through downed timber up the steep climb. If you want to get to these lakes, the easiest way may be from between Jet and Shadow Lakes, but it will require navigating by map and compass. The slope is much easier this way, though.

Past the two lakes, the trail continues a gentle descent, through timber and across open meadows. As you pass the nose of a north-south ridge, you begin a climb taking you to Crater Lake. It sits on a shelf below Blair Mountain. From here, the trail ascends, using switchbacks to make the climb easier until you reach the top of the limestone wall. The Crater Lake Trailhead is one-half mile west, down the open slope.

Trails Outside the Wilderness

In addition to the trails within the Flat Tops Wilderness, there are many others in the surrounding area. The trails listed here take you into roadless areas, although a few included here do permit the use of bikes and ATVs at certain times of the year. A portion of Routt National Forest north of County Road 8 was once included in proposed additions to the Wilderness. As with the Wilderness trails, this listing begins at Meeker and follows a clockwise direction around the Flat Tops.

This listing does not include all roadless-area trails surrounding the Flat Tops, but those that follow have some wilderness-like character. Many tend to receive less use than wilderness trails.

RIO BLANCO COUNTY ROAD 8
(Forest Road 8)
LOST CREEK TRAIL 1808

Description

The trail follows Lost Creek north, staying in the bottom of the stream's small canyon. At three miles, it connects with a trail that leaves Forest Road 230 from the south. For a loop trip, head south here to the road, then pick up Trail 1809 a mile farther south at Long Park and return to the trailhead. Otherwise, you can continue north to Trail 1805, one more mile.

Destination

Lost Park, Trail 1805

Distance

5 miles

Elevation

7,600, 8,390

Directions to trailhead

Ten miles east of Buford on County Road 8, to Lost Creek Guard Station, then one-half mile east to parking area at Long Lost Trailhead.

Maps

Lost Park

LOST PARK TRAIL 1805

Description

From its junction with Trail 1808, this trail has two forks. The west fork goes north four miles to Trail 1114 in Salt Park. The east fork goes north two miles to Trail 1113. Connecting trails can be used to make a loop trip back to Trail 1808.

Destination

Trail 1114, Trail 1113

Distance

4 or 2 miles

Elevation

8,390 at junction, 9,520 at Salt Park, 9,100 at Trail 1113

Directions to trail

From Long Lost Trailhead, 5 miles north on Trail 1808.

Maps

Lost Park, Slide Creek

WILLIAMS FORK TRAIL 1113

Description

From Trail 1805E, the trail heads northeast into the head-waters of the South Fork of the Williams Fork. It follows the stream north to Forest Road 990.

Destination

Trail 1114 and South Fork of the Williams Fork, FR 990

Distance

3, 5 miles

Elevation

9,100 at Trail 1805E, 7,720 at Forest Road 990

Directions to trail

Connects with Trail 1805E at the Routt-White River National Forest boundary. Also, it can be accessed from the north from Moffat County Road 55 and Forest Road 990.

Maps

Lost Park, Slide Creek

TRAIL 1114

Description

The trail follows Corral Creek east to the confluence of the South Fork of the Williams Fork. In Salt Park, at the junction with Trail 1805, you'll find many ponds and creeks.

Destination

Trail 1113

Distance

5 miles

Elevation

10,100 one mile north of Sleepy Cat Peak, 8,080 at Trail 1113

Directions to trailhead

North, five miles on Trail 1808 to Trail 1805W, then four miles north. Also, from Forest Road 990, two miles south on Trail 113.

Maps

Sleepy Cat Peak, Slide Creek

SNELL CREEK TRAIL 1810

Description

Follows Snell Creek, a small stream, for three miles up Snell Canyon. The trail crosses the creek in an open meadow, then heads northwest, then follows the slope, staying in the open most of the next four miles to the junction of Trail 1804.

Destination

Trail 1804

Distance

6 miles

Elevation

8,370 at trailhead, 10,060 at Trail 1804

Directions to trailhead

Six miles east of Long Lost Trailhead on Forest Road 8 (Rio Blanco County 8)

Maps

Ripple Creek

PAGODA LAKE TRAIL 1804

Description

This is an easy hike through scattered timber, open parks, and wetlands. Good camps sites are available. To the north, you have a view of Pagoda Peak, which appears much like the pagodas of Asia.

Destination

Pagoda Lake, Trail 1195, Trail 1810, Forest Road 230

Distance

4, 5, 6, 9 miles

Elevation

10,276 at Trailhead, 10,630 at Sand Peak, 10,401 at Forest Road 230

Directions to trailhead

One-quarter mile west of Ripple Creek Pass on Rio Blanco County Road 8 (Forest Road 8)

Maps

Lost Park, Pagoda Peak, Ripple Creek

RIO BLANCO COUNTY ROAD 8
(Forest Road 16)
TRAIL 1112

Description

This trail crosses several small eastward-flowing creeks. The relatively low elevation allows an easy hike over varied terrain. Should be a good place to see deer and elk.

Destination

Forest Road 970

Distance

6 miles

Elevation

9,100 at trailhead, 9,293 near Harp Point

Directions to trailhead

Five miles east of Ripple Creek Pass on CR 8 (FR 16), then one mile north on Forest Road 969

Maps

Pagoda Peak

ROUTT COUNTY ROAD 7
(Forest Road 900)
HEART LAKE TRAIL 1110

Description

The trail is a part of the Ute Trail, once used by the Indians travelling in this area.

Destination

Bull Park Reservoir, McChivvis Reservoir, Heart Lake

Distance

5, 5 1/2, 6 miles

Elevation

9,385 at trailhead, 10,000 at Moody Creek, 9,380 at Bull Park Reservoir

Directions to trailhead

10.5 miles west of Yampa on CR 7.

Maps

Orno Peak

SUNNYSIDE LAKES TRAIL 1861

Description

The walk to the Sunnyside Lakes is easy, with little change in elevation. South, past the lakes, the route begins climbing. At the junction one-half mile south of the lakes, go west. From here, the trail climbs, working its way around the head of Cabin Creek Basin. The terrain is rugged. You can see Dome Peak a mile to the west.

Destination

Sunnyside Lakes, Trail 1877, Trail 1860

Distance

3, 6, 7 miles

Elevation

9,890 at trailhead, 10,690 1 mile from Trail 1860

Directions to trailhead

From Forest Road 900 nine miles west of Yampa, south on Forest Road 910 past Gardner Park Reservoir to junction of Forest Road 915, then south to Egeria Creek and trailhead.

Maps

Dome Peak, Orno Peak

Several trails in the following areas were once traveled by the Ute Indians.

EAGLE COUNTY ROAD 301
INDIAN CLIFFS TRAIL 1877

Description

Most of this trail leads through open, arid, rugged county. Take plenty of water. At Trail 1860, go south to Forest Road 610 to make a seven-mile loop trip.

Destination

Trail 1860

Distance

4 miles

Elevation

9,520 at trailhead, 10,200 at Forest Road 610

Directions to trailhead

Begins from Forest Road 610, two miles from the junction of Forest Road 612

Maps

Dome Peak

CANARD CREEK TRAIL 1837

Description

The trail follows the Middle Fork of Derby Creek southeast two miles, then crosses the creek. It then heads uphill along the nose of the ridge for a mile. At the fork in the trail, go left or south, one mile to Forest Road 613. For a six-mile loop trip back to the Middle Derby Trailhead, at the trail junction go west one-half mile to the South Fork of Derby Creek and Trail 1836.

Destination
   Forest Road 613
Distance
   4 miles
Elevation
   8,600 at Middle Derby Trailhead, 9,160 at Forest Road 613
Directions to trailhead
   From Burns, west on Eagle County Road 39, seven miles to Forest Road 610. West on Forest Road 610, four miles to Forest Road 612. Take left fork, Forest Road 612, one mile to trailhead.
Maps
   Dome Peak

BEAR PARK TRAIL 1836

Description
   The trail climbs a steep ridge as it heads southwest to a ridgetop park. Past the meadow, the trail crosses the ridge as it wanders through timber, then descends to the South Fork of Derby Creek. At the trail junction by the creek, go west to Forest Road 613, or east to Trail 1837 and return to Middle Derby Trailhead. Distance for this loop trip is seven miles.
Destination
   South Fork of Derby Creek
Distance
   3 miles
Elevation
   8,600 at Middle Derby Trailhead, 9,060 at Forest Road 613
Directions to trailhead
   From Burns, west on Eagle County Road 39, seven miles to Forest Road 610. West on Forest Road 610, four miles to Forest Road 612. Take left fork, Forest Road 612, one mile to trailhead.

EAST FORK TRAIL 2177

Description
   The trail climbs west to cross a saddle, then descends to the East Fork of Derby Creek, the only source of water near the trail. Just east of the creek, you come to a trail junction. The west fork joins Trail 2073, one-half mile west. The right fork connects with the same trail one-half mile farther north. The walk takes you through open country having small stands of timber.

Destination
    Trail 2073
Distance
    2 miles
Elevation
    8,280 at Forest Road 611, 9,300 at Trail 2073
Directions to trailhead
    From Eagle County Road 301, six miles southwest from Derby
    Junction, northwest on Forest Road 611 to trail.
Maps
    Sugarloaf Mountain

RED DIRT TRAIL 2073

Description
    The trail heads southwest, crosses the East Fork of Derby Creek,
    then ascends a small drainage gulch heading west. It contin-
    ues climbing to a small flat with small ponds in small mead-
    ows. Here, the trail heads north to connect with Trail 2177, or
    you can continue north to Forest Road 616.
Destination
    Trail 2177, Forest Road 616
Distance
    5 miles
Elevation
    8,100 at Forest Road 611, 9,500 at Forest Road 616
Directions to trailhead
    From Eagle County Road 301 five miles southwest from Derby
    Junction, northwest on Forest Road 611 to trail
Maps
    Sugarloaf Mountain

WEST FORK TRAIL

Description
    This one follows the West Fork of Red Dirt Creek through rug-
    ged terrain.
Destination
    Trail 2032
Distance
    5 miles
Elevation
    7,100 at Forest Road 611, 9,720 at Trail 2032

Directions to trailhead

From Eagle County Road 301, three miles southwest from Derby Junction, northwest on Forest Road 611 to trail.

Maps

Sugarloaf Mountain

UTE-SWEETWATER TRAIL 2032

Description

This trail heads northeast below the flanks of the Flat Tops Wilderness. It connects with several trails that give access to the Wilderness. It also joins trails that wander the arid country south and east the plateau. The Forest Service says this was one of the travel routes of the Ute Indians. The trail can be hiked from either trailhead.

Destination

Big Spring Trailhead

Distance

9 miles

Elevation

7,750 at Sweetwater Guard Station, 9,570 at Big Spring Trailhead

Directions to trailhead

West on Eagle County Road 40, ten miles to Sweetwater Guard Station.

Maps

Sugarloaf Mountain, Sweetwater Lake

TRAIL 1839

Description

This is a short trail that connects two trails that lead into the Wilderness from the Sweetwater Lake area. The easiest access is from the Turret Creek Trailhead. It crosses Turret Creek, then climbs the arid, open east side of a rugged canyon to connect with Trail 2067.

Destination

Trail 2067

Distance

3 miles

Elevation

8,260 at Trail 1832, 9,950 at Trail 2067

Directions to trail

From the Turret Creek Trailhead, two miles west of Sweetwater Lake, north one mile on Trail 1832.

Maps

Sweetwater Lake

CROSSING TRAIL 1855

Description

This is part of a network of trails leading west and south from the Sweetwater Lake Campground. It heads west up a steep ridge above the lake, giving a good view of the Sweetwater Creek drainage.

Destination

Trail 1854

Distance

7 miles

Elevation

7,700 at Sweetwater Lake Campground, 9,400 at Trail 1854

Directions to trail

West from Sweetwater Lake Campground

Maps

Deep Lake, Sweetwater Lake

FOREST ROAD 600
BROKEN RIB TRAIL 1849

Description

The trail follows Broken Rib Creek, leading down into a steep-sided canyon to Grizzly Creek. Rugged country but the scenery is beautiful.

Destination

Trail 2065 and Grizzly Creek, Forest Road 631

Distance

2, 5 miles

Elevation

10,150 at Broken Rib Spring, 8,950 at Grizzly Creek

Directions to trailhead

Eighteen miles on Forest Road 600 from Eagle County Road 301, to Broken Rib Spring and parking area.

Maps

Broken Rib Creek, Carbonate

GRIZZLY CREEK TRAIL 2065 (North)

Description

The trail follows Grizzly Creek from its head on the flats, downstream through an increasingly rugged, challenging canyon. Camp sites are available through the canyon until the walls begin to close in the last two miles of the trail, at the south end. You'll pass ponds, springs, and waterfalls along the trail.

Destination

Trail 1849, end of trail

Distance

5, 9 miles

Elevation

10,360 at Grizzly Cow Camp, 8,000 near falls above Grizzly Creek

Directions to trailhead

Twenty-one miles on Forest Road 600 from Eagle County Road 301, to Forest Road 632, then west four miles on the four-wheel-drive road to Grizzly Cow Camp.

Maps

Broken Rib Creek, Carbonate

HANGING LAKE TRAIL 1851

Description

This short trail takes you to a popular scenic area.

Destination

Hanging Lake, Bridal Veil Falls

Distance

1 1/2 miles

Elevation

6,150 at trailhead, 7,200 at Hanging Lake

Directions to trailhead

In Glenwood Canyon seven miles west from Dotsero, or nine miles east from Glenwood Springs on Interstate 70 to Hanging Lake Exit. Currently, access is only from the east bound lanes.

Maps

Shoshone

GRIZZLY CREEK TRAIL 2065 (South)

Description

The trail follows Grizzly Creek upstream from its confluence with the Colorado River. It is located in the bottom of a deep, rugged canyon.

Destination

Trail 1847

Distance

5 miles

Elevation

5,950 at trailhead, 8,640 between Grizzly and No Name Creeks, 7,840 at Trail 1847

Directions to trailhead

In Glenwood Canyon, eleven miles west from Dotsero, or five miles east from Glenwood Springs on Interstate 70 to Grizzly Creek Trailhead.

Maps

Glenwood Springs, Shoshone

NO NAME CREEK TRAIL 1847

Description

The first 5 miles wander north at the bottom of another deep canyon. Past East No Name Trail, the terrain becomes more open and less difficult. A rugged, challenging loop trip can be made by hiking north to Trail 2065, where you will climb a steep saddle to cross over into Grizzly Creek. Take this trail back to Interstate 70, then follow the people path back to No Name. Total distance is eleven miles.

Destination

Trail 2065, Trail 1849, Forest Road 602

Distance

3, 5, 7 miles

Elevation

7,840 at Trail 2065, 8,960 at Trail 1849, 9,895 at Forest Road 602

Directions to trailhead

In Glenwood Canyon fourteen miles west from Dotsero, or two miles east from Glenwood Springs on Interstate 70 to No Name Exit. Take road north one-half mile to gate

Maps

Glenwood Springs

Appendix
Federal Agencies

Bureau of Land Management
2850 Youngfield
Wheat Ridge, CO 80033
(303) 239-3600

U.S. Fish & Wildlife
Denver Regional Office
134 Union Blvd
Lakewood, CO 80228
(303) 236-7904

U.S. Forest Service
Rocky Mountain Regional Office
730 Simms
Lakewood, CO 80228
(303) 275-5350

White River National Forest
Supervisor
Old Federal Building
PO Box 848
Glenwood Springs, CO 81601
(303) 945-2521

Blanco Ranger District
(White River NF)
317 E. Market
PO Box 358
Meeker, CO 81641
(303) 878-4039

Eagle Ranger District (White River NF)
125 W. 5th St.
PO Box 720
Eagle, CO 81631
(303) 328-6388

Rifle Ranger District (White River NF)
0094 County Road 244
Rifle, CO 81650
(303) 625-2371

U.S. Geological Survey
7.5 Minute topograpic
quads and other maps
PO Box 25286
Denver Federal Center, BLDG. 810
Lakewood, CO 80225
(303) 236-7477

Yampa Ranger District (Routt NF)
Routt National Forest
300 Roselawn
PO Box 7
Yampa, CO 80483
(303) 638-4516

WILDERNESS BUSINESSES and SERVICES

Adams Lodge
2400 County Road 12
Meeker, CO 81641
(303) 878-4312
Cabins, meals, horse rentals, guided
wilderness trips

Buford Store
County Roads 8 & 17
Buford, CO
Limited groceries, gas, propane, fishing tackle

Fritzlan's Guest Ranch
1891 County Road 12
Meeker, CO 81641
(303) 878-4845
Cabins, restaurant, horse rentals,
guided wilderness trips

Pollard's Ute Lodge
393 County Road 75
Meeker, CO 81641
(303) 878-4669
Cabins, RV and tent spaces,
horse rentals, guided wilderness
trips, private fishing

Ripple Creek Lodge
39020 County Road 8
Meeker, CO 81641
(303) 878-4725
For year-round information:
3495 S. Pierce St.
Denver, CO 80227
(303) 989-4950
(303) 989-5818 (FAX)
Cabins, family style meals, horse rentals, guided wilderness trips, fishing and hunting licenses

Trappers Lake Lodge
16064 County Road 8
Meeker, CO 81641
(303) 878-3336
Cabins, family style meals, horse rentals, guided wilderness trips, guided fishing, boat rentals on Trappers Lake, convenience store, fishing tackle, fishing and hunting licenses

White River Resort
PO Box 1107
Eagle, CO 81631
(303) 690-6627 (Radio Phone)
Cabins, family style meals, horse rentals, guided wilderness trips
For year-round information:
21679 E. Otero Pl.
Aurora, CO 80016
(303) 690-6627

Bibliography

Bass, N. Wood and Northrop, Stuart A. *Geology of Glenwood Springs Quadrangle and Vicinity Northwestern Colorado*, Geological Survey Bulletin 1142-J, Washington, DC, 1963.

Chronic, Halka. *Roadside Geology of Colorado*, Mountain Press Publishing Co., Missoula, MT, 1980

Cole, David N. *Low-Impact Recreational Practices for Wilderness and Backcountry*. U.S. Department of Agriculture - Forest Service General Technical Report INT-265, Ogden, UT 1989

Kloepfer, Deanne and Marsh, Susan, eds. *Keeping it Wild - A Citizen Guide to Wilderness Management*. The Wilderness Society and USDA Forest Service, Washington DC, 1992

Ubbelohde, Carl, Benson, Maxine, and Smith, Duane A., eds. *A Colorado History*. Pruett Publishing Co., Boulder, CO, 1982

LEAVE NO TRACE Outdoor Skills & Ethics, National Outdoor Leadership School, Lander, WY, 1992

Horse Sense - Packing Lightly on Your National Forests, USDA Forest Service

Index

—End—

HAY

BAR - H

800- 230- HUNT